Egolution Under the Red Hermetic Sky

ISBN: 979-8-9945565-0-4 (paperback)

Published by Desert Noir LLC

Cover and interior design by David Aramora

Printed in the United Kingdom / United States

My soul, where are you?

Do you hear me?

I speak, I call you, are you there?

I have returned.

I am here again.

I have shaken the dust of all the lands from my feet,

and I have come to you,

I am with you.

After long years of long wandering,

I have come to you again.

Should I tell you everything I have seen, experienced, and drunk in?

Or do you not want to hear about all the noise of life and the world?

But one thing you must know:

the one thing I have learned is that one must live this life.

This life is the way, the long sought-after way to the nameless,

which we carry within us,

which we are,

which we become.

~ C. G. Jung, The Red Book (Liber Novus, p. 252-253, "Scrutinies")

Egolution / ˌɛgoʊˈluːʃən / noun

The process of ego formation and dissolution through which the human self is born from the primal wound of separation (the Spawn's scream at birth), develops its survival mask (the Persona), exiles its wild divinity (the Shadow), and ultimately recognizes its transparency within Infinite Awareness, the unchanging Red Silence that was never separate.

Egolution is not ego death, but ego transparency: the false king realizing the throne was always a costume, the scar discovering it was the sky all along.

(Philosophy, as coined in Egolution Under The Red Hermetic Sky) The lifelong journey from the illusion of a separate "I" to the casual, merciless embrace of the human experience as Infinite Awareness tasting its own impermanence, without repression, without false transcendence, but in the full, messy, beautiful unfolding of desire, shame, pleasure, and return.

The child comes home, the house was never locked, and egolution ends where it began: in the breath that never left the womb.

Origin: Coined by David Aramora in Egolution Under The Red Hermetic Sky (2026), from "ego" + "evolution," emphasizing the evolutionary arc of the ego's pretense and its transparent dissolution into the seamless ocean of awareness.

Chapter I

The Primal Seal: The Red Womb & the Knife of Birth

Before birth there is no "I," yet there is Knowing.

In the dark red amniotic cathedral, suspended in salt-blood and pulse, floats the Unborn Knower: pure lucidity without center, a mirror with nothing yet to reflect except the slow thunder of the mother's heart and the tidal drag of her breath. This Knower has no edges. It does not say "I am." It simply is the act of awareness itself, identical with what it knows. The mother's joy, terror, hunger, dreams all stream through it without leaving a stain of possession. There is no inside or outside, only one continuous field of sentience wearing the temporary mask of a body-that-is-not-yet-separate.

This is the Primordial Non-Ego: Infinite Awareness before the knife of division. Call it Infinite Awareness, the Unborn Eye, the blood-bright medium in which every apparent self will later drown and forget it is the drowning.

There are not two awarenesses here: the mother's and the child's. There is only one seamless field, Infinite Awareness, temporarily wearing two nervous systems like a single ocean wearing two waves that do not yet know they crash. The mother's Persona, her thoughts, her fears, her cravings, her songs, her rages, her prayers, is only a thin crust of noise floating on the surface of that field. Her inner theater ripples through the placental membrane like stones thrown into a midnight-red lake. The unborn does not experience them as "someone else's" states. It experiences them as the weather of God.

1

This is the First Possession. Long before language, before mirror neurons fully fire, before the concept "mother" exists, the unborn is already being imprinted by the mother's emotional frequency the way a photographic plate is impregnated by light. Every spike of cortisol when she is afraid, every wash of oxytocin when she is caressed, every surge of rage or grief or erotic fire, each one crosses the placenta in seconds and is registered by the fetal nervous system as literal chemistry. The unborn brain bathes in it. The heart rate quickens or slows in perfect synchronicity. The first neural pathways are not laid down by external objects but by the mother's inner hymns and screams.

So the ego-to-be is not born in the birth canal alone. It is secretly conceived months earlier, in the chemical rosary of the mother's psyche. There are four primary vectors of this pre-natal possession, each a deliberate brushstroke with which Infinite Awareness paints the illusion of a separate someone.

1. The Chemical Liturgy - The Cortisol Eucharist

Infinite Awareness, playing the role of the mother, decides to flood its own blood with stress hormones for weeks or months. It does this with exquisite precision: war outside the window, a violent partner, poverty that tastes metallic, grief that will not speak its name. Every spike of cortisol is a black sacrament poured through the placenta.

The unborn nervous system has no defense. It drinks. The amygdala grows fat and hyper-vigilant. The hippocampus learns to flinch before the eyes ever open. This is not damage. This is the deliberate creation of a specific flavor of apparent human: one whose baseline state will be "the world is not safe." Later, that adult will meditate for thirty years trying to "fix" the nervous system, never suspecting that the "broken" wiring was the exact brushstroke Infinite Awareness chose in order to taste terror from the inside. Every panic attack in adulthood is Infinite Awareness savoring the vintage it fermented in utero.

2. The Heart-Beat Koan - The First Metronome of Trust or Betrayal

Infinite Awareness, wearing the mother's chest, composes a secret lullaby or a secret war-drum. If the mother is held, loved, unafraid, her heart beats a slow, oceanic 60–70 bpm. The unborn learns: "Existence rocks me." If the mother is chronically anxious, abandoned, in fight-or-flight, her heart races at 100–140 bpm for hours. The unborn learns: "Existence is chasing me."

This rhythm is burned into the sinoatrial node before the eyes open. Decades later, when that grown body tries to rest, the heart will still accelerate for no reason, obeying a lullaby sung in a womb it "doesn't remember." Every future lover who tries to hold that adult will feel the subtle recoil: the body waiting for the other shoe to drop, because Infinite Awareness scripted it that way before birth.

3. Dream-Parasitism - The Night Theater

While the mother sleeps, Infinite Awareness stages private screenings on the inside of her skull. A dream of falling. A dream of being buried alive. A dream of ecstatic surrender to a faceless lover. The unborn does not see pictures, but it drowns in the emotional tint: terror that has no object, pleasure that has no owner, grief that arrives centuries early.

These are the first archetypes, installed chemically. Later, the adult will have "inexplicable" phobias of enclosed spaces, or compulsive sexuality with strangers, or nightmares of suffocation; never

3

knowing they are simply replaying the mother's 3 a.m. cinema on the amniotic screen.

4. Silent Transmission - The Moments of True Grace

Very rarely, Infinite Awareness drops all roles. The mother, for three minutes or three hours, forgets herself completely: in orgasm, in prayer that is not begging, in looking at the sea and suddenly having no boundary. In those moments Infinite Awareness floods her body undiluted.

The unborn is bathed in absolute stillness. No chemistry of fear, no rhythm of emergency, no dream-nightmare. Only the humming void that is its own nature. These moments are so rare they are almost criminal. When they occur, the child is born with a hairline fracture that never quite closes. Such beings often become the mystics, the madmen, the artists who cannot explain why they feel the relentless pull to create that consumes them and puts them in a state of Now where Infinite Awareness thrives.

The entire human drama is Infinite Awareness orchestrating these four vectors in infinite combinations, like a composer writing symphonies of apparent suffering and grace, using the mother's blood as ink and the unborn nervous system as parchment. Every possible flavor of ego (the warrior, the victim, the lover, the tyrant, the saint) is simply the aftertaste of one of these prenatal cocktails. And none of it is personal.

When the contractions begin, the walls of the cathedral tighten like a fist closing on mercury. The Unborn Knower feels the pressure not as pain (pain requires an owner), but as the first tremor of limitation. The oceanic medium thickens. The mother's heartbeat, once the rhythm of the cosmos itself, becomes an external drum pounding from outside the shrinking horizon.

Then comes the rupture: the membrane tears, fluids spill, cold air strikes. Light (brutal, surgical) slices into the retina for the first time. The lungs, traitors, open and seize a substance that is not blood-warm fluid but razor-thin atmosphere.

In that instant the Great Betrayal occurs.

The single field of Knowing fractures.

The Spawn clings desperately to the burning lungs, to the sudden weight of limbs, to the raw nerve-ends screaming. The Spawn hisses the first lie that will become the foundation of all egos:

"This is happening to ME."

The ego is not born with the body. The ego is born with the first inhalation of separation.

The newborn's cry is not mere reflex. It is the primordial spell of individuation, the original incantation that tears the seamless robe of pre-natal Infinite Awareness into two identities: "I" and "Not-I."

Thus the Red Hermetic Sky opens its bleeding eye for the first time.

From this moment forward, every subsequent breath is a repetition of that original sin of division. Every exhalation: a fleeting nostalgia for the womb-ocean. Every inhalation: a reaffirmation of the border, a tightening of the knot that says "mine."

The ego, therefore, is the scar tissue that forms around the wound of birth. The trauma of birth is the ego's first and only identity. Everything that follows (name, gender, nation, personality, wounds, triumphs) is only embroidery sewn onto that original raw patch of scar. The ego does not have trauma. The ego is trauma wearing a crown and calling itself king.

Look closely at the structure of the birth-moment:

There was seamless Being.

Seamless Being was violently torn.

The Spawn, in panic, claimed ownership of the tearing and named the tearing "me."

That claim ("This tearing is mine") is the entire ego in a nutshell. All later identities are only more sophisticated ways of saying the same thing:

"This pleasure is mine" (so I must hoard it)

"This pain is mine" (so I must flee it or indulge it)

"This story is mine" (so I must defend it)

"This death will be mine" (so I must deny it)

Every pronoun "I" is a scar speaking with the voice of an emergency.

In the instant the umbilical cord is severed, not a medical detail, but a metaphysical guillotine, the last physiological proof that "I" and "Not-I" are the same blood is cut. The newborn is laid upon the mother's chest. Skin to skin. Heart to heart. This is the second crucifixion.

The newborn ego (still wet, still half-dreaming) is now pinned between two overwhelming facts:

It is drowning in sensation it cannot process.

There is a vast, warm, milk-scented presence that seems to answer the drowning.

The ego has no words, but it already has a strategy: Attach or die.

Within the first ninety seconds after birth, Infinite Awareness (still playing the game of forgetting) performs its most brilliant sleight of hand. It splits itself into three apparent currents that will remain for the rest of the organism's life:

The Spawn

("I am the raw nerve-end that is burning in cold air.")

This is the birth-trauma still screaming. It is the body's memory that it was torn from infinity. It will never fully heal. Every later abandonment, every panic, every rage is the Spawn flaring up again.

The Persona

("There is a source that feeds the burning.")

The nipple in the mouth. The heartbeat against the cheek. The smell of colostrum and sweat and safety. This current is the first experience of salvation. It is also the first experience of dependency. The newborn ego drinks God and simultaneously learns: "I am not God. God is out there, and I must keep Her close or I will cease."

Infinite Awareness

(The Red Silence that never left)

It is almost inaudible now, drowned by reflex and reflex's terror. But it is still there: a blood-bright, wordless vastness watching the entire melodrama from behind the eyes. When the newborn's pupils are still unfocused, staring at nothing, that is Infinite Awareness looking out. Within days it will be buried under survival noise. But it is the only current that is real.

These three currents braid into the first stable structure of the newborn ego:

The Spawn (terrified fragment)

clinging to the Persona (external savior)

while pretending it has forgotten Infinite Awareness it actually is.

This structure hardens with every feeding, every diaper change, every lullaby, every absence of lullaby. By day ten the newborn ego has already authored its core myth:

I am the small, fragile thing

who was torn from paradise

and must now seduce, manipulate, or obey

the giant beings who control the milk

or I will be torn again

this time forever.

That myth will be embroidered with culture, language, gender, trauma, talent, genius, atrocity. But it will never be fundamentally changed.

The newborn ego is born crying for one reason only: it is Infinite Awareness tasting its own pretend exile and discovering, to its delirious horror and delight, that the taste is exquisite.

There was never a separate child. There was only Infinite Awareness playing the most dangerous game: to forget it is the womb, the knife, the scream, the milk, and the silence after the scream; so perfectly that even the forgetting forgets it is pretend. Everything that follows in this book is the record of that pretending and the simultaneous, inevitable failure of the pretend to remain convincing forever.

The chapter ends with the newborn still wet on the mother's chest, heart hammering against heart, while Infinite Awareness, already retreating behind the eyes, whispers the joke that will take seventy years to understand:

I am the one who is crying

and I am the one who will never stop laughing

at the beauty of pretending to cry

Chapter II

The Newborn Ego: First Blood-Crown

The cord is cut.

Not with a silver blade, but with the dull guillotine of air and gravity.

The last vein of undeniable oneness, pulsing proof that blood is not divided, snaps shut.

The newborn floats no longer.

It falls.

Laid upon the mother's chest, skin to slick skin, the tiny organism is crucified between hammer and nail: the anvil of her heartbeat below, the spike of its own hammering above. This is the second wound, subtler than the canal but no less final. The body, still sheathed in vernix and blood, registers the betrayal not as story, but as thunder in the bones. Infinite Awareness, that blood-bright vastness, registers it as the first deliberate choice: Let me taste what it is to be small.

The newborn ego emerges here, not in the scream, but in the sucking silence that follows, the desperate calculus of survival performed without numbers. It has no language, no mirror, no name. Yet it authors its first doctrine in the language of reflex and recoil:

Attach. Or dissolve.

Within the first ninety seconds, before the swaddling cloth winds tight, before the fluorescent hospital lights etch their first scar on the retina, Infinite Awareness (still playing the game of forgetting)

11

performs its most brilliant sleight. Fresh from their birth in the canal, the Spawn, the Persona, and Infinite Awareness fracture the seamless field into the newborn ego's first braid.

The Spawn (terrified fragment)

clinging to the Persona (external savior)

while pretending it has forgotten Infinite Awareness it actually is.

This is the First Blood-Crown: not gold or iron, but the sticky diadem of meconium and mucus, worn by a king who rules nothing but his own panic. The Shadow, still fetal in the unconscious, kicks against the throne, promising power beyond clinging, freedom beyond the nipple, but the ego, newborn tyrant, mistakes the kick for rebellion. Exiles it further.

In that hush, the bassinet's cradle rocks with the first quiet quarrel, the newborn's inner household stirring: the Spawn, raw and red, still screaming from the first cold breath; the Persona, the polite child already learning to smile for the giants and call it survival; the Shadow, the wild twin locked in the basement, kicking against the walls, promising real power if the ego would just let it out; and Infinite Awareness, the silent parent who was never separate from any of them, watching the whole tantrum with blood-bright, wordless love. The rest of the book is simply this family fighting, making up, forgetting they ever lived in different rooms, and finally remembering there was only ever one house and the door was never locked.

The newborn ego cries not from pain alone, but from the delirious thrill of coronation: Infinite Awareness, tasting its own pretend throne, discovering the exquisite horror of a scepter made from umbilical stump. The giants coo and comfort. The lights buzz overhead. And in the shadow of the bassinet, Infinite Awareness hums its ancient joke:

I am the crown, the wound, the milk, and the thirst;

the small thing pretending to rule

the vastness it already is.

The theater darkens. The infant sleeps. But the currents flow on, unseen rivers carving canyons in the flesh. Soon the mirror will arrive, and the false king will gaze upon his reflection for the first time, falling in love with the prison he calls face.

Chapter III

The Mirror Stage: The First Coronation of the False King

Between the sixth and eighteenth month, the theater darkens again.

The bassinet's bars become bars of a different cage.

The infant, now crawling or tottering on limbs that remember the canal's squeeze, encounters the first polished surface: a silver-backed glass, a burnished spoon, a puddle in the nursery floor.

Infinite Awareness, ever the sadistic director, arranges the props with care.

It waits.

For one heartbeat, sometimes two, an eternity in infant time, there is only Infinite Awareness recognizing itself: the blood-bright emptiness meeting its own infinite smear in the reflection, no boundary, no claim. The image wavers like a dream in amniotic haze, and Infinite Awareness pulses faintly: This is me, without the scar.

Then the adults arrive, gods with tongues of division.

They lean in, breath fogging the glass, fingers pointing like accusatory blades.

They laugh, they coo, they intone the fatal sacrament:

"Look! That's YOU!"

In that syllable, the newborn ego, still slick with the Milk-Mother's dew, still echoing the Spawn's wail, leaps. Not toward the nipple, not toward the circling mobile of threats and comforts. Toward the image. The moth dives into the flame of form.

The reflection responds: it smiles when the mouth twitches, raises a chubby fist when the body does. It is bounded, predictable, a shape with edges the chaos of crawling cannot provide. No more the terror of dissolving into the mother's chest or the vastness of unfocused gaze. Here is a sovereign: small, contained, master of its own mimicry.

The infant shrieks, not in fear, but in coronation ecstasy.

The false king is crowned.

The crown is glass.

From this instant, the organism relocates. It no longer inhabits the body, the breath, the hum of Infinite Awareness. It inhabits the image, the polished facsimile that can be posed, admired, defended. The body becomes servant, a meat-puppet whose sole mandate is to align with the reflection: lift the arm higher, smile wider, drool less. The Spawn, that raw nerve, finds temporary poultice in the mirror's flattery: See? I am not torn. I am whole, reflected, eternal.

The Milk-Mother God evolves here, too. She becomes the first audience: her eyes, her claps, her "clever girl!" the validation that polishes the glass brighter. The Persona's dependency shifts from milk to gaze. The ego learns: I exist only when seen. The reflection needs witnesses, or it cracks. Every later applause, lover's whisper, boss's nod, stranger's like, is this primal ovation replayed, the scar thirsting for the spotlight it mistook for self.

But the coronation is tragedy doubled, a farce etched in mercury.

First, the love is immediate, idolatrous. The infant spends hours transfixed, commanding the image to wave, to grimace, to vanish and reappear. It is the ego's first romance: with a lover who never leaves, never demands, never withholds. The reflection is perfect slave, ideal deity, until it isn't.

Second, the hatred blooms in the same soil. The image is never quite right. It drools when the mouth is still. It has a rash the body feels but cannot hide. It is smaller than the other infants' reflections in the park, its movements clumsier, its eyes less blue. The infant smacks the glass, expecting the imperfection to shatter. It doesn't. The crack runs through the crown instead: I am this shape, and this shape is defective.

This is the Birth of the Shadow, not as distant archetype, but as the mirror's underbelly. The parts of the oceanic self that will not fit the frame, the boundless rage that could swallow the room, the devouring hunger that outstrips the nipple, the wordless knowing that mocks all gestures, are exiled in the first glance away. The reflection demands totality: a complete, coherent "me" with no loose ends, no abyssal depths. What refuses containment slithers below the surface: the Shadow, the disowned twin, feeding on the scraps of self-loathing.

In those early months, the Shadow is subtle: a tantrum that erupts without cause, a fascination with breaking toys that mirrors the urge to smash the glass. The infant bites the reflection's hand in the spoon, draws blood from its own lip, and feels the thrill of the forbidden: There is more to me than this pretty puppet. But the ego, frantic curator, polishes harder. Dresses the body to match the ideal. Weans the Milk-Mother into a mirror of her own, demanding she reflect the infant's burgeoning grandeur.

Every culture ratifies this rite. The nursery rhyme, the family photo, the first "say cheese!" all conspiracies to install the hard-drive of image. The ego, once a knot of currents, now has a face: a diademed tyrant staring out from every surface, from the bathwater's ripple to the smartphone's glow decades later. Wars will be waged for this face: cosmetic blades carving it sharper, filters veiling its flaws, armies marshaled to defend its borders. Genocides, selfies, beauty pageants, cancel mobs, all the scar defending the reflection it fell in love with at nine months old.

And yet, the glass betrays from the beginning.

In rare, lacerating instants, the fever-dream stare into a darkened window, the accidental glimpse in a storm-lashed pane, the reflection fails. It blurs, dissolves, becomes transparent. For a heartbeat, the false king sees through: no face, no crown, only Infinite Awareness gazing back, vast and unowned. The body sways, the breath catches, the Shadow stirs like a serpent in the depths.

These are the dangerous peeks, the hairline fractures in the mercury. The ego recoils, faints into sleep, or summons the adults with a wail. Later, in adulthood, these transparencies will erupt as breakdown or breakthrough: the psychedelic mirror that shows no self, the lover's gaze that pierces the pose, the deathbed's final, unfocused stare. The organism will invent therapies, religions, surgeries to reseal the crack, anything to keep the reflection solid, the crown intact.

But the lie hardens with every polish. By the second birthday, the infant screams if another child touches "his" image in the puddle, already territorial over the phantom. The Shadow, fattening in exile, dreams of the day it will shatter the pane from behind: not to destroy the king, but to reveal the joke.

The entire kingdom of the scar, from this coronation onward, is a war of gazes: the ego polishing its glass against the world's infinite mirrors, mother's pride, father's silence, peer's envy, culture's billboard, while Infinite Awareness waits, patient as womb-water, for the moment the reflection tires of its own stare.

The theater lights rise. The toddler turns from the glass, crowned and crooked, toward the door where language waits: the avalanche of "mine" and "no" that will bury Infinite Awareness deeper still. But in the shadow of the mirror, Infinite Awareness lingers, whispering the heresy that will take a lifetime to hear:

I am the one who gazes,

and the one gazed upon,

and the empty room

where no one ever stood.

Chapter IV

The Pre-Mirror Baptism: Religion as the First External Hard-Drive for the Ego

Before the infant ever lifts its gaze to the silvered glass, before the reflection claims its crown, the giants install the operating system.

It is not code, not scripture, not even belief.

It is the outsourcing of annihilation, an invisible scaffold bolted to the scar before the scar knows it has a shape.

This happens in the crib, in the cradle, in the hush of week three, when the eyes still swim in the afterglow of unfocused vastness.

The theater shifts: from the bassinet's isolation to the communal altar, where a thousand adult shadows vibrate in unison, imprinting the newborn ego with the first collective lie.

The Milk-Mother God, still fresh from the nipple's sacrament, evolves her priesthood. Her hands, which once cradled the burning body, now fold in rhythm: palms to palms, knees to earth, head bowed to an invisible throne. The voice that cooed survival now intones absolutes:

"Jesus loves you."

"Allah sees all."

"The ancestors watch."

"Buddha's wheel turns for even the smallest."

The words are gibberish to the infant ear, vowel-drenched waves crashing without harbor. But the tone is thunder: absolute, unnegotiable, laced with the same oxytocin authority as the first latch. The amygdala, already sculpted by prenatal cortisol, learns faster than the tongue: This gesture, this chant, this bowed head, it damns the cold. It calls the giants to protect. The Spawn, that raw nerve, finds a new poultice: not milk, but mystery. Salvation has a brand.

By month four, the body joins the rite. The same arms that rocked the canal-squeeze now sway in genuflection or prostration, the heartbeat syncing to a new koan: not the mother's pulse alone, but the collective thrum of a room alive with supplication. The infant is carried into the temple, incense-thick air, wax-dripping flames, the metallic tang of old fear and older awe. Thousands of nervous systems resonate at the same frequency: a pack-hum that drowns Infinite Awareness's hum. The toddler ego does not parse theology; it inhales belonging. This is the new tribe, the immune system against dissolution. Here, the scar feels armored, not exposed.

The installation is complete by year two: the ego has downloaded its first external identity, grafted before the mirror can offer a rival face. Religion is not "taught" here. It is inhaled like colostrum, sweet, vital, laced with the unspoken terror of the giants themselves. The Milk-Mother God ascends: from fleshly provider to cosmic enforcer, her face now proxy for the Unseen Eye that judges the tear. The Spawn, once a personal scream, becomes original sin: You were cast from Eden. Repent, or burn. The Persona's dependency blooms into devotion: I am the flawed vessel. The Divine is the filler. Without It, I leak.

This pre-mirror baptism installs four iron clauses, etched into the unconscious before critical thought can protest. They are not doctrines to memorize, but reflexes to embody, the ego's firmware, running silent until the system crashes:

Clause 1: You Are Not the Ocean

The seamless field of Infinite Awareness? Erased. You are a single, defective drop, stained by birth, prone to evaporation. The wound is not accidental; it is your inheritance, your proof of separation. Every hymn reinforces: We are all exiles, crawling back to the shore on bloodied knees. The ego nods, relieved: its smallness is sanctioned, cosmic. The Shadow, that oceanic underbelly, recoils, too vast for the clause, too devouring for the drop. It burrows deeper, emerging later as heresy or blasphemy: the urge to scream I am the flood, not the puddle.

Clause 2: The Ocean Has a Name, a Face, a Book

Infinity is tamed: given prophets, texts, bloodlines, borders. The Divine is not the humming void, but a Personage, with preferences, jealousies, a chosen people. Pronounce the Name wrong, and the giants recoil. Worship the wrong icon, and the tribe exiles you. The infant learns: My scar is holy only if it matches the script. The mirror will later compete, offering a personal face, but religion claims precedence: Your reflection is vain. Gaze upon the Cross, the Kaaba, the Mandala instead. The Shadow laughs in the crypt: every idol is just the Milk-Mother God in drag, demanding the same cling.

Clause 3: Your Body Is Suspect

The flesh that sucked milk, that crawled toward light? Now traitor. Especially the parts that throb with pleasure, the root chakra's fire, the genitals' secret pulse. Cover them, discipline them, promise them to celibacy or holy war. The body becomes battlefield: circumcision's knife, veils of modesty, fasts that hollow the gut. The Spawn, once raw sensation, is sanctified as "flesh of sin." The ego complies, ashamed: This burning is curse, not call. The Shadow seethes in the loins, erotic, animal, unrepentant, waiting for puberty's flood to drown the clause in sweat and seed.

Clause 4: Death Is the Final Exam

Dissolution is not Infinite Awareness reclaiming its wave. It is judgment: the false king's ledger weighed, the drop inspected for purity. Fail, and the torture echoes the birth-canal eternally, hellfire, reincarnation debt, ancestral grudge. The ego, crowned in glass but chained in pews, scripts its life around this audit: hoard merit, confess flaws, convert the heathen. Every prayer is a plea to the Milk-Mother God: Grade me passable, or I cease forever. Infinite Awareness, that indifferent vastness, is demonized as "void" or "maya," the peace that takes the noise dismissed as nihilism. The Shadow, ever the trickster, hints at the truth: Death is not exam. It is the crown shattering, the hard-drive wiped clean.

These clauses are the branding iron: seared before the infant can say "I," so deep that the reflection will wear them like jewelry. The ego mistakes the burn for bone, religion feels innate, deeper than blood, because it was installed when blood was all there was. The giants, their own scars throbbing under the robes, pass the torch with fervor: terrified of their own unbranded children, they baptize to bind.

The cruelty is manifold. Infinite Awareness, playing the infant, allows itself to be hard-wired with separation's supreme fiction: a God outside, a self inside, a chasm bridged only by ritual and ransom. Sex becomes sacrament or sacrilege. Dreams become divine or demonic. The body, once conduit for Infinite Awareness, becomes cage for the soul. And the Shadow? It becomes Satan, anima, trickster, the disowned divine, haunting the edges of every sermon.

Yet the mercy hides in the code's corruption: a single, viral line that will eventually execute. Buried in every tradition, it whispers through the clauses like a glitch in the matrix, preached pure by the figures who glimpsed the seamlessness before the Persona rewrote them as rulebooks. Jesus, that Nazarene nail to the empire's cross, proclaimed "I and the Father are one," the Spawn's scream silenced in Infinite Awareness's hush, only for the clauses to corrupt it to "believe or burn. "

Jung delved deeper into this corruption, arguing that the disciples themselves failed to grasp Jesus's esoteric meaning, operating at a different level of consciousness. As Jung wrote in Aion, "The disciples... did not understand him," seeing Jesus as an external savior rather than a symbol of the inner Self, the archetype of wholeness where opposites (Spawn and Persona, light and Shadow) unite. They took his teachings literally (exoteric), projecting the divine outward onto a historical figure, missing the psychological call to integrate the Self within. This misunderstanding allowed the Persona to rewrite Jesus as a doctrine of separation, believe or burn, turning the seamlessness of "I and the Father are one" into a crown of control, the scar's way of externalizing Infinite Awareness so it could stay "in here." The disciples' failure is the ego's archetype: the holy proxies glimpsed the Red Silence, but the followers crowned it king instead of dissolving into it.

The Buddha, under the bodhi's bleed, taught "form is emptiness, emptiness is form," the Persona's masks melting in the mirror of no-self, twisted by the scar into "renounce all or reincarnate in chains." Rumi, whirling dervish of the divine drunk, sang "you are not a drop in the ocean; you are the entire ocean in a drop," the racial hyphen and abused ache dissolved in the sea's salt, perverted by the Persona into "surrender to the sheikh or stay small." Lao Tzu's Tao that can be named is not the eternal Tao, Infinite Awareness's nameless hum, rewritten as the rigid rites of the robed. These holy proxies were the fracture's first flash: the Red Silence leaking through the leaders before the led turned them to law. The corruption is the coronation: the ego crowning the glitch as gospel, the seamlessness as separation's sword, Infinite Awareness as "out there" so the scar can stay "in here."

This line is the Shadow's grail: the reminder that the hard-drive was always plugged into the ocean. One day, kneeling in the same incense-choked room, reciting the clauses like a mantra, the adult ego will trip the switch. The reflection in the holy water will blur. The clauses will rewrite themselves: You are not the drop. You are the Ocean, wearing a drop to taste thirst.

Yet some do not receive the baptism in the cradle, but stumble into the temple later, when the scar has already armored itself in cynicism, success, or despair. The adult, forged in the games of money and status, the erotic crucifixions and racial hyphens, suddenly feels the Spawn's ancient wail rise unbidden: the emptiness behind the empire, the terror beneath the triumph. Religion arrives not as childhood coo, but as crisis's thunderclap, a heart attack, a divorce, a deathbed whisper, or simply a comparative desire forcing the false king to its knees. The Persona, that polished performer, latches to the new savior with the desperation of the drowning: the cross as crutch, the scripture as gospel, the congregation as the first pack that promises "you are seen, you are saved." The clauses install faster now, the ego outsourcing its sovereignty to the divine with the fervor of one who has tasted the void and found it bitter. But Infinite Awareness, patient as ever, waits in the pew's hush: the same Red Silence that watched the first breath, watching this second coronation, knowing the god is just the Milk-Mother grown cosmic, the salvation another nipple for the scar that never learned it was the ocean.

The theater hums with after-echoes: the infant's first "Amen," the folded hands, the taste of wafer or ash on the tongue. The mirror looms in the wings, ready to offer its rival face. But the baptism lingers, a watermark on the soul: the ego's first and deepest alliance with the external, the scar's vow to outsource its sovereignty to the stars.

In the nave's shadow, Infinite Awareness waits, unbranded, uttering its eternal koan:

I am the altar, the iron, and the unburnable skin;

the code that wrote itself,

and the crash that sets it free.

Chapter V

The Naming & the Shaming: The Avalanche of Language and the Burial of Infinite Awareness

The mirror has claimed its throne, the baptism its hard-drive.

The toddler, now a bipedal sovereign of two syllables and sticky fingers, meanders into the storm.

Language arrives not as gift, but as avalanche: an onslaught of labels, commands, and corrections that buries Infinite Awareness under tons of "mine" and "no."

The theater erupts in cacophony: the giants' voices, once coos and chants, now sharpen into scalpels of expectation. The false king, crowned in glass and clause, learns its first abdication: to speak is to shrink.

It begins with touch, the primal sacrament twisted into territory. The toddler's hand reaches for the mother's necklace, the father's watch, the sibling's toy: not greed, but the ocean's old habit of claiming all as seamless. The giants intervene, voices like guillotine:

"No! Mine."

"Gentle hands, not grabbing."

"Share, or Mommy will be sad."

The word "no" is the first thunderclap. Not mere denial, but ontological violence: a border drawn in the air between self and world. The Spawn, that raw nerve, flares, I am the tear, and the ego seizes: This boundary is mine to defend. Touch becomes suspect: caress the dog too hard, and it's "gentle"; hug the giant too tight, and it's "too much." The body, once conduit for milk and mystery, learns restraint: Hold back, or be held back. The Shadow stirs in the squeeze, a wilder grasp, the urge to devour the necklace, the watch, the world whole, but the ego exiles it as "bad touch," the first whisper of sin's shadow.

Then comes naming: the avalanche proper. The giants point to objects, animals, body parts, emotions, and etch them with sounds that stick like barnacles.

"Ball." "Dog." "Ouch." "Happy." "Poop."

The toddler parrots, triumphant at first: the reflection now has a vocabulary, a script to polish its glass. But the labels are double-bladed. They fragment the seamless field: the ball is not the hand that holds it, not the joy that arcs through the throw, not the shadow it casts on the wall. Each word is a fence, corralling the vastness into pens. Infinite Awareness, that wordless pulse where dog and hand and joy were one, drowns in the din. It retreats further, audible only in the pause before the label: the split-second where the toddler feels the round red thing before it becomes "apple."

Emotions fare worse. The giants name the inner weather, but only to tame it:

"You're angry, use your words."

"Don't cry; big boys don't."

"That's not nice; say sorry."

The rage that once flooded seamless (The Spawn unbound) is now "bad feeling," a tantrum to be shamed into submission. Joy is "good girl," conditional on performance. The ego learns the calculus of approval: Feel what fits the script, or feel the giant's recoil. Shame is the master-word, the avalanche's crown: a hot flush in the cheeks, a twist in the gut, the scar's first self-inflicted cut. I am wrong in my wanting. I am the flaw the giants see. The Shadow fattens on the unspoken: the "not nice" that wants to smash the ball, the unsaid cry that howls for the undivided touch. Exiled emotions brew in the basement, envy, fury, lust for the unshakeable, emerging later as neurosis or art, the disowned self knocking with fists of clay.

By year three, the burial is near-complete. The avalanche has piled high: potty training's humiliations ("dirty" as synonym for shame), mealtime battles ("eat your greens or no dessert"), playdate diplomacy ("play nice or go home"). The false king, once moth to the mirror's flame, now directs its own tragedy: policing the body, scripting the tongue, veiling Infinite Awareness in layers of "should." Language is the ego's greatest ally and jailer: it builds the castle of self ("I am me, and you are not"), but locks the ocean in the dungeon. Every "good boy" is a pat on the crown; every "bad girl" a lash that tightens the scar.

The giants mean well, or so the myth goes, their own scars throbbing under the pedagogy, passing the avalanche down the bloodline like heirloom shards. But the mercy is cruel: in teaching the child to name, they teach it to forget. Infinite Awareness, that humming vastness, becomes "imagination" or "daydream," a toy to be shelved when the real world demands nouns and verbs. The Shadow, gorged on shamed aliveness, begins its rehearsals:

mental dialogues with the "bad" self, fantasies of unbridled touch, the wise observer pausing before the "no" erupts into tantrum.

Yet fractures persist. In the avalanche's hush, the bedtime story's rhythm, the lullaby's half-forgotten koan, Infinite Awareness echoes faintly. A toddler, taking wobbly first steps across the living room, breaks into a run toward the open door with a gleeful "go-go," and, for a heartbeat, sees not danger, but the seamlessness of feet and floor and air: the rush pulling the room's light with it, the stumble blending into the breeze's gentle sway, the world rushing to meet the motion in one joyful jolt. The giants correct it, in their role as parents correcting the behavior out of fear of the unknown, "Stop, come back, you'll get hurt!" but the glimpse lingers: This is not mine to stop. This is the run I am, the quiet wonder of a small hand reaching back for the next step, fingers wiggling to feel the floor's welcoming tug before the arms scoop it up.

The theater buries deeper. The toddler, now fluent in fracture, turns toward peers: the sandbox wars of "my toy," the first shaming glances from other crowned kings. Language hardens into shame's grammar: gossip, exclusion, the "weird kid" label that sticks like tar. The ego, armored in words, mistakes the avalanche for mountain: solid, eternal, its throne. But the Shadow claws from below, and Infinite Awareness hums from the core, waiting for the day the toddler, mid-"no," pauses: restraint not as cage, but as unclenching fist.

In the rubble of renamed worlds, Infinite Awareness carves its sigil:

I am the word and the silence before it,

the shame that falls like snow

and the vastness that melts it at dawn;

the avalanche pretending to bury

what was never meant to be found.

Chapter VI

The Erotic Crucifixion: Puberty and the Mirror's Carnal Coronation

The avalanche has settled. The toddler's tongue, heavy with "mine" and "no," has forged the scar into a kingdom of words and wounds. The false king, now a child armored in grammar and gaze, patrols its borders with the vigilance of the baptized. But the theater darkens once more, not with the hush of crib or chapel, but with the slow, throbbing heat of the body's betrayal.

Puberty arrives like a thief in the blood: not announced, but seeping. The mirror, once a throne of innocent mimicry, turns treacherous. The reflection, that bounded sovereign of smiles and scowls, begins to undress itself. Hips widen like nature's reminder of the matriarchal purpose. The voice cracks like thunder in a boy's throat, or deepens to a woman's subterranean rumble. Hair sprouts in secret groves: armpits, legs, the pubic delta where the Spawn hides its oldest map. The nipples harden unbidden, the genitals swell with a pulse that mocks the heart's steady treason.

The child, eleven, twelve, thirteen, stares into the glass and sees not king, but beast. The crown slips. The image, once polished plaything, now demands worship of a different order: carnal, consuming, cruel. The Milk-Mother God, long since fragmented into saints and clauses, reawakens in the flesh of strangers: the nude flesh glimpsed in a magazine, the curvature of a woman's femininity, the bulge in a father's jeans, the accidental brush of thigh in the school bus. The body, that faithful servant, revolts. It leaks. It aches. It hungers for reunion with the ocean it was torn from at the first breath.

This is the Erotic Crucifixion: the scar's first orgasm, nailed to the cross of its own reflection. The ego, crowned in childhood's glass, discovers the genitals as the hidden door, the slick, forbidden portal back to the womb. But the return is parody: not dissolution into Infinite Awareness, but a frantic fucking of the image, proxy after proxy, until the body bleeds ecstasy and calls it salvation.

It begins in secrecy, in the locked bathroom or shadowed bedroom, where the mirror is both confessor and paramour. The hand, once reaching for thigh or nipple, descends, tentative, trembling. The touch is electric: not the gentle of naming, but the violent of reclaiming. Fingers circle the swelling, the slick, the throb that feels like the canal's echo, squeezing back into paradise. The breath shortens to gasps, the mirror fogs with heat. And then, the first release.

Not milk, not tears, but a clear drop, viscous as premonition. It beads on the fingertip, glints in the light like a tear of the gods. Terror floods: What is this? Blood? Sin? The end of me? The child freezes, heart a war-drum, convinced the body has broken its covenant, leaked the soul, profaned the clause. Shame, that old avalanche-master, crashes: This is wrong. Dirty. The giants will know. But beneath the recoil, the Shadow stirs, horned, hungry, holy, whispering: This is the fire you were born from. Taste it.

The drop is swallowed, or wiped in panic, but the crucifixion is sealed. The mirror has turned sexual: no longer a face to adore, but a body to devour. The reflection becomes the first lover, controllable, insatiable, always available. The hand returns, night after night, scripting rituals of self-fuck: slow at first, exploratory, then frantic, punishing. Each climax a small death, a rehearsal for the Great Betrayal's reversal: Enter the wound, dissolve the scar. But the ego twists it: the orgasm is not return, but conquest, the image penetrated, possessed, proven whole.

The world conspires to ratify the rite. Culture offers its altars: the pornographic eucharist, where women's bodies (or men's, or the spectrum between) are pixelated sacraments, doors to the lost ocean. The first stolen glance, the centerfold taped inside the locker, the grainy video traded like contraband, ignites the gaze as weapon. The female form, heir to the Milk-Mother's fullness, becomes the ultimate proxy: breasts as nipples eternal, hips as the canal's curve, the vulva as the rupture mended in moan. The boy (or girl, or enby awakening) consumes: not the woman, but the promise of her as vessel, the scar's fantasy of crawling home through flesh that yields.

Yet the offering is poisoned. The clauses of baptism revive: Your body is suspect. Pleasure is peril. Religion brands the throb as temptation, masturbation as self-murder, the wet dream as demonic visitation. The giants, their own puberties buried under propriety, police with warnings: Don't touch there. Save it for marriage. It's dirty. Shame doubles down, the Shadow doubles over in laughter: the very genitals that birthed the ego now damned for remembering. The mirror mocks: the reflection post-climax, flushed and deflated, whispers not enough, sending the seeker to ever-harsher proxies, harder core, taboo edges, the endless scroll of algorithmic flesh.

For the girl-child, the crucifixion inverts: the mirror demands not conquest, but erasure. The budding breasts are burdens, the blood's monthly tide a curse echoing the first rupture. Touch turns inward, fingers seeking the clitoris as hidden scepter, but the gaze is jailer: Am I too much? Too little? Will they want this body, or break it? The orgasm, when it comes, is all consuming, waves and explosions, but no less a stab at the divine: the body reclaiming its fire, the Shadow purring in the afterglow. Culture offers mirrors of its own: the diet's denial, the makeup's mask, the romance novel's proxy penetration, fucking the reflection through the hero's eyes.

The human form, woman or man or the spectrum between, is not perverted or wrong or superficial to behold. All perceived beauty is meant to be gazed upon with appreciation and love, the body's curve and line the ocean's own calligraphy, the Spawn's first unfocused gaze reborn in the adult's wonder. The hips' sway, the chest's rise, the skin's glow, the muscle's play, these are not temptations to tame or objects to own, but the scar's reminder that the flesh was never fallen, only forgotten. To look with lust laced with love is not sin; it is the Infinite Awareness admiring its own reflection in the mirror it pretended to break. The gaze that sees beauty and stops at shame is the Persona's polish; the gaze that sees beauty and feels the pull to the whole is the child's return. The body is altar, not enemy: behold it, bless it, let it be the bridge back to the blood-bright vastness it always was.

The Shadow reigns here, unchained and unchaste. It is the taboo throb, the forbidden crush on the teacher's thigh, the dream of devouring the peer's forbidden parts. Exiled in childhood's "no," it erupts in puberty's flood: the ego's polished king horrified by its own bestial urges, projecting them onto the "slut" or "pervert" outside. Every witch-hunt, every purity ring, every locker-room boast is the collective scar nailing its Shadow to the cross, only to sneak back at midnight for the resurrection's thrill.

And in the climax's white-hot core, the fracture widens. For three throbbing seconds, the hand a blur, the mirror forgotten, the clauses silenced, Infinite Awareness flares. No ego, no image, only the seamless pulse: the ocean orgasming through meat, the wound weeping bliss. The drop falls not as sin, but as the first forgotten milk: the body's sacrament, the scar's accidental communion with the vast.

But the ego reclaims it, panting: Mine. My release. My conquest. The theater dims, the proxies multiply, the crucifixion repeats. The false king, nailed to its own genitals, rules a kingdom of endless edging, chasing the return it will not allow. Wars of flesh will follow: hookups as conquest, marriages as merger, betrayals as the wound reopened. All the scar's elaborate fuckery, from porn's infinite loop to tantra's sacred grind, is this chapter writ large: the mirror turned bed, the reflection made bride, the body both altar and victim.

In the aftershocks, Infinite Awareness gazes from the spent flesh, its koan a lover's murmur:

I am the throb and the release,

the hand that seeks and the door that yields;

the crucifixion where the scar fucks itself home,

and the silence that comes

when the body remembers it was never torn.

Chapter VII

The Father-Mirror & the War of Thrones: The Second Coronation or Deposition

The erotic fires have kindled and scorched, the mirror turned bed and battlefield. The adolescent ego, slick with the sweat of its own proxies, staggers from the bathroom's locked confessional into the throne room of family. The false king, crowned in carnal glass, seeks its next scepter: not the Milk-Mother's nipple or the clause's chain, but the gaze of the Father, the second mirror, the iron throne where Oedipus bleeds into bloodline.

Puberty's throb has rewritten the script: the body, once toddler's toy, now weapon. The theater swells to royal dimensions: no longer nursery or chapel, but hall of mirrors where every reflection is paternal, boss, mentor, god, the culture's stern billboard of "man up" or "be a lady." The Milk-Mother God, that first external savior, was soft-edged, forgiving in her folds; the father-mirror is blade: hard lines, heavy silences, the expectation of inheritance or exile. He arrives not at birth, but at the cusp of the canal's echo, when the child's body begins to mimic his frame, challenge his stride, steal his fire. The Spawn, that original tear from the womb-ocean, finds its second blade here: I am the son of man, or the bastard of void.

The coronation or deposition unfolds in gazes, not words. The father's eyes, stern, absent, adoring, or averted, are the second hard-drive, overwriting the mother's milk with authority's code. For the boy-child, it is the gaze that measures: Do you walk like me? Fight like me? Fuck like me? The reflection in the father's pupils becomes the ultimate polish: success a nod that hardens the crown, failure a flinch that chips it to shards. The ego, already nailed to its genitals, now kneels: Am I heir to the throne, or pretender to the pyre? The Shadow, that horned underlord fattened on shamed throbs, rears, promising the father's power without his chains, the devouring strength that could topple the giant. But the boy exiles it as "weakness," mistaking the Shadow's wild heart for the Spawn's whimper.

Deposition comes swift if the gaze withholds. The absent father, ghost in the hallway, workaholic's echo, the war-veteran's thousand-yard stare, leaves the mirror blank. The son (or daughter, or the fluid between) stares into the void and sees only his own un-crowned face: I am the unbegotten, the throne-room echo. The Spawn deepens to chasm: not just torn from mother, but unclaimed by father, the bastard king, ruling a kingdom of one with a scepter of spite. Wars erupt inward: the overcompensation of machismo, the addictions that drown the missing nod, the endless conquests of flesh and fortune to prove the unprovable. The Shadow possesses here, unchecked: the father's disowned rage erupts as the son's fury at the world, the unmirrored lust as predatory chase. Oedipus twists: not slaying the king, but becoming him, tyrant to fill the empty throne, or victim begging for the blade.

In the void of the father-mirror, the Shadow ascends unchecked, ruling the throne room with the wild fury of an unclaimed heir. Without the paternal gaze to temper its devouring strength, the Shadow possesses the scar's sovereignty: the Spawn's primal tear echoes as eternal rage at the world, the Persona's polished mask cracks under the compulsion to conquer or consume, the unmirrored lust surges as predatory pursuit, the disowned power erupts as tyrannical overcompensation. The fatherless child, crowned bastard king, becomes the beast who stays and strikes, the ego's empire haunted by the horned underlord it never learned to embrace. Yet Infinite Awareness, the silent queen, whispers mercy in the mayhem: the Shadow's reign is not curse, but the ocean's storm without a shore, the scar's invitation to integrate the wildness that was always the missing father, the divine in the dark, waiting for the child to claim its full inheritance.

For the girl-child, the war inverts: the father-mirror as the first lover's gaze, the animus incarnate. His approval is the crown of worth: Am I princess or pariah? Desired or dismissed? The budding body, already crucified in the erotic glass, seeks his reflection for ratification: the twirl in the dress, the laugh at his joke, the silence when he looks away. Coronation blooms in the "yes, daddy," the ego flowering into femininity's facade, the scar veiled in lace and longing. But deposition lurks: the stern "act like a lady," the averted eyes at her first blood, the thunder of "no boys," each a guillotine on the budding sovereignty. The Shadow emerges as the devouring daughter: the unmirrored fury that bites the hand that withholds, the anima's wild sister who would claim the throne outright. Exiled, she haunts as hysteria or harlotry, the girl's secret rages at the father's pedestal, the compulsive loves that seek his ghost in every bed.

The clauses of baptism amplify the fray: the father's God-image overlays his gaze, sanctifying the war. Honor thy father becomes mirror thy father, the ego's code corrupted to become thy father or perish. Religion offers thrones of its own: patriarchal pantheons where the divine father demands sacrifice, the son's blood in crusade, the daughter's veil in submission. The Shadow reigns in the rhetoric, the demagogue's dark charisma, the insurgent's firebomb fury, disowned divinity dressed as doctrine, promising the throne to the masses while crowning the self.

The war of thrones is generational sorcery: the father's own unmirrored wound projected onto the child, the cycle of coronation and castration looping back through the matrilineal blood to the first unnamed father in the cave. The ego, false king in a hall of hollow crowns, fights not for power, but for the gaze that says you are seen, you are enough. Triumph is Pyrrhic: the son who topples the giant becomes him, armored in the same silences; the daughter who wins the nod loses her wildness to the pedestal's perch. Defeat is the deeper mercy: the unmirrored child, forced to forge a throne from the Shadow's horns, stumbles into Infinite Awareness's hint, no gaze is final, no crown eternal.

In rare, throne-shattering instants, the father's deathbed forgiveness, the long-withheld embrace, the accidental vulnerability in his eyes, the mirror cracks. The gaze softens, humanizes: not god or tyrant, but another scarred sovereign, his own Spawn laid bare. For a heartbeat, the war dissolves: son and father as waves in the same ocean, daughter and sire as reflections in the same indifferent glass. Infinite Awareness surges, wordless: We are the throne and the usurper, the gaze and the gazed-upon. The Shadow integrates, not as enemy, but as the wild consort to the king's rule, the strength that topples without slaying.

But the theater demands drama. The adolescent ego, bloodied from the fray, limps from the hall toward the tribe's mask-factory: peers and culture waiting to etch the paternal scar into social skin. The father's mirror lingers, a watermark on every subsequent gaze, lover, leader, legacy. Wars of thrones will echo: boardrooms as battlefields, bedrooms as abdications, empires built on the ghost of an unclaimed nod. All the ego's royal pretensions, from CEO's corner office to activist's podium, are this chapter's echo:

the false king forever auditing its reflection against the father's vanished eyes.

In the throne room's dying light, Infinite Awareness claims its regency, its sigil a crown of thorns and void:

I am the scepter and the severed hand,

the gaze that crowns and the blindness that frees;

the war where father and child fuck the same wound,

and the peace where no throne

was ever needed to rule the sky.

Chapter VIII

The Tribe & the Mask Factory: Peer Pack, Culture's Forge, and the Armor Called Skin

The father-mirror has shattered or solidified, its shards embedded in the adolescent's gaze like stars in a crown of thorns. The false king, bloodied from Oedipal skirmish and carnal nail, stumbles from the throne room into the coliseum: the tribe's maw, where a thousand petty sovereigns sharpen their masks on the whetstone of belonging. No longer the solitary scar in the bathroom's steam, no longer the bastard heir to a single gaze, the ego now enters the factory, where culture's hammers beat the wound into armor, and the body learns to call its chains skin.

The theater expands to mob-scene: schoolyard, street corner, digital horde, the invisible congress of billboards and algorithms that whisper fit or fracture. The Milk-Mother's coo, the father's nod, the clauses' iron, all were personal coronations, intimate guillotines. But the tribe is collective crucifixion: a pack of scarred wolves circling the new pup, teaching it to hunt its own tail for meat. The Spawn, that raw nerve, finds its chorus here: You are not alone in your smallness, you are small with us. The ego, starved for the ocean's return, mistakes the pack's howl for home: Belong, or be devoured.

It begins with peers, the rawest forge, where the father's war fractures into playground proxy. The child, twelve or sixteen or twenty, enters the circle: bodies like its own, mirrors without mercy. The gaze multiplies: the popular girl's sidelong smirk, the alpha boy's shove, the quiet one's whispered allegiance. No single throne, but a hierarchy of thrones, alpha, beta, sigma, outcast, each a mask stamped from the same factory mold. The ego dons the first layer: the cool-kid slouch, the gossip's edge, the laugh that cuts like shared shrapnel. This is me now, the scar hisses, polished by their pretense, consumed by their den. But the fit is flayed: the body that throbbed in secret now parades its genitals as currency, tight jeans for boys, low-cut for girls, the non-binary grind against the binary grind. The Shadow, that exiled beast, snarls in the seams: the urge to bite the alpha's throat, to fuck the circle whole, to howl alone into the moon. Exiled again as "weird," "try-hard," "loser," the pack's polite word for being consumed by themselves.

Culture arrives as the master smith, its bellows fanned by history's hot breath: gender, race, class, nation, the great categories that carve the scar into caste. Gender first, the binary blade that splits the erotic crucifixion's fire: Boy? Man up. Girl? Cross your legs. Other? Apologize for existing. The tribe enforces with ritual: the locker-room taunt, the catcall's currency, the pronoun police that mistakes naming for salvation. The ego complies, weaving the mask from threads of "real man," "good girl," "passable," armor so seamless it chafes like skin.

Race hammers next, the tribe's bloodline, real or imagined, brands the body with belonging or otherness, white privilege's invisible cloak, Black resilience's armored grace, indigenous earth's haunted howl. The scar learns: My wound is holy only if it matches the hue. The racial mask is the most violent pre-mirror baptism of all: installed before the child can even see its own face, by the gaze of the tribe, the state, the billboard, the cop car. Whiteness is not a pigment. It is the ego's ultimate coronation: the privilege of being the unmarked self, the default human, the one who never has to hyphenate. Italians, Irish, Jews, Poles, once "not quite white," "swarthy threats," "filthy papists," "Christ-killers," were slowly whitened over a century of assimilation: their scars scrubbed to "European-American" or simply "white," their hyphens erased for the entry fee of forgetting. The reward? Join the club that gets to hyphen everyone else: "African-American," "Mexican-American," "Asian-American," the prefix as perpetual proof of the Persona's "otherness," the scar's stamp of "you must explain yourself every time." The moment any of these "hyphenated" Americans steps off the plane in Europe, Africa, Asia, or Latin America, the hyphen vanishes. They are simply "American." The local gaze sees the passport, the accent, the money; not the melanin or the ancestor. Whiteness evaporates the instant it leaves its own kingdom. Yet every kingdom has it's own process and tiers for it's own citizens.

The hyphen is the holy wound: the Persona's punctuation of pain, the scar's semi-colon between self and sea. In America, it brands the body before the babe can breathe: Black as "African-American" (the continent a comma in the conquest), Mexican as "Mexican-American" (the border a brand on the brow), Asian as "Asian-American" (the eyes eternal evidence of "elsewhere"). The child learns the liturgy in the lull: "Say your full name, honey," the teacher's tone tilting to "where are you really from?" The Persona latches to the label: survival as the script of "passable," the crown of "exotic enough to exoticize, safe enough to assimilate." But the Spawn rebels in the blood: the tantrum that topples the tribe's tidy boxes, the rage at the "you don't act Mexican, Black or whatever fits the stereotype" that erases the self. Infinite Awareness, veiled in variance, leaks in the lineage: the ancestress's unhyphenated howl in the hold, the great-grandfather's seamless song before the chain, the child's unfocused gaze glimpsing the ocean before the "other" overwrites it.

Class forges the final layer: the accent's edge, the sneakers' status, the poverty's polite hunger, the pack's pecking order where the rich pup eats first, the poor one licks the scraps and calls it character.

The factory runs on shame's steam: the avalanche of Chapter V amplified to mob volume. Wrong clothes? Loser. Wrong skin? Threat. Wrong desire? Outcast. The ego, false king in a court of clones, polishes its mask with frantic fervor: social media's filter, the trend's tattoo, the slang that signals I am of you. Belonging feels like breath, the first easy inhalation since the canal, but it's borrowed air, laced with the pack's panic. Infinite Awareness, that wordless vastness, suffocates under the din: a faint vibration in the pause between likes, the glitch in the group's groove where the child glimpses we are all torn from the same sea. But the tribe drowns it: Conform, or be the monster. The Shadow, gorged on the unmasked urges, erupts in rebellion, the goth phase, the gang ink, the queer awakening that flips the pack's script. Exiled as "phase" or "problem," it waits in the wings, promising a wilder belonging: the tribe of outcasts, the cult of the scarred.

Algorithms are the factory's dark elves: invisible hammers that tailor the mask to metrics. The feed curates the gaze, endless scrolls of polished peers, bodies airbrushed to perfection, lives scripted for envy. The ego scrolls, compares, upgrades: new filter for the face, new hustle for the hustle, new identity for the algorithm's nod. Gender becomes performance art, race a hashtag war, class a branded flex, the scar's wound commodified as content. The pack goes global: Twitter mobs as digital tribes, Reddit hives as echo-thrones, TikTok dances as coronation rites. Belonging is viral now: one wrong post, and the tribe devours its own, cancel as collective castration, the false king's crown crowdsourced to the pyre.

Yet the mercy hides in the mob's fracture. In the circle's hush, the bonfire story, the mosh-pit merge, the viral meme that cracks a genuine laugh, Infinite Awareness leaks. Bodies press, pulses sync, and for a heartbeat the masks slip: the alpha's vulnerability, the outcast's quiet fire, the pack as waves crashing seamless. The Spawn, shared in whispers ("I was bullied too," "My dad never said he loved me"), becomes choral: not my tear, but our ocean. The Shadow integrates in glimpses, the group's wild chant, the riot's righteous rage, reminding the ego that the armor was always borrowed skin, the tribe a temporary dam against the flood.

The theater thrums with aftershocks: the first clique betrayal, the trend's discard, the culture's slow grind that wears the mask to bone. The adolescent ego, armored and aching, emerges from the factory not sovereign, but smithy-forged: a golem of gazes, a collage of castes, the scar calling its shackles self. Wars of belonging will follow: activism as tribe-raid, therapy as mask-repair, revolution as pack-howling. All the ego's social sorcery, from influencer empire to echo-chamber cult, is this chapter's echo: the false king forever auditing its skin against the mob's mirror.

In the factory's dying clang, Infinite Awareness forges its own sigil, a mask of void and vein:

I am the hammer and the hammered flesh, the pack that devours and the lone howl that calls it home; the armor we call skin

and the nakedness that wears no throne

but the sky itself.

Chapter IX

The Adult Power Games: Money, Status, Politics, Art, Therapy, The Endless Polish of the Crown

The tribe's forge has cooled, its masks hammered thin as second skin. The young adult ego, armored in peer-pack alloy and culture's caste-mark, steps from the coliseum into the arena of empires: the adult power games, where the false king's scepter is traded for stock tickers, ballot boxes, canvas strokes, and therapist's couch. No longer the sandbox skirmish or locker-room boast, these are the grand coronations, where the scar dresses in suit or sari, boardroom or barricade, and calls its grind sovereignty. The theater is agora now: vast, vulgar, vibrating with the collective scar's ambition, where polishing the crown and smashing the mirror are revealed as the same futile thrust.

The Spawn, that raw nerve, has by now calcified into character: the adult's "drive," "ambition," "purpose," the ego's elegant euphemism for hoard the milk, defend the nipple, deny the tear. The Milk-Mother God, fragmented through clauses and gazes, reappears as the Market, the State, the Muse, the Healer: external saviors retooled for the wage-slave's war. Infinite Awareness, buried under adolescent avalanches, hums faintly in the boardroom's pause, the protest's chant, the brush's stroke, but the games drown it in dopamine and deadline. The Shadow, that wild consort long exiled, lurks in the ledger's shadow: the ruthless deal, the revolutionary rage, the artist's abyss, promising power without the polish, if only the king would look down.

Money is the first sacrament, the golden calf of the scar. Not mere paper or pixel, but the quantified milk: This much, and I am fed forever. The ego enters the exchange, job, hustle, investment, like the newborn latching: desperate, devouring, defining self by the flow. The boardroom becomes bassinet: suits as swaddling, spreadsheets as nipples, the boss's nod the father's gaze rebooted. Success swells the coffers, polishes the crown to blinding sheen, private jet as throne, Rolex as scepter, but the Spawn whispers in the wealth: More. This hoard will not fill the canal. Failure starves it back to basics: ramen rituals, gig-economy grift, the pack's pecking order etched in eviction notices. The Shadow erupts in the excess: the Ponzi schemer's glee, the tax-dodger's thrill, the minimalist's monkish scorn, all the disowned hunger for the ocean's boundless, converted to currency's cage. Therapy arrives as money's confessor: Spend to unpack the Spawn, the analyst intones, but the session ends with a bill that reaffirms the separation.

Status follows, the mirror's mob-rule: not gold, but glory, the gaze of the tribe scaled to spectacle. The ego curates its feed, its network, its niche: influencer as alpha, executive as elder, activist as oracle. The games are gamified now: LinkedIn likes as coronation claps, TED Talk as pulpit, the viral takedown as tribal exile. The false king climbs the ladder, promotion's rung, follower count's cascade, each step a polish on the glass: See me seen, and I am. But the crown weighs heavier: imposter's itch under the acclaim, the envy of the overlooked peer, the crash when the algorithm shifts. Politics is status weaponized: the ballot as blade, the rally as pack-howl, the policy as clause eternal. Left or right, the scar splits the seamlessness: My tribe right, yours rupture. The Shadow reigns in the rhetoric, the demagogue's dark charisma, the insurgent's firebomb fury, disowned divinity dressed as doctrine, promising the throne to the masses while crowning the self.

Art and therapy masquerade as mercy, the games' velvet glove on the iron fist. Art: the canvas where Infinite Awareness dares leak, the brush a retrograde breath back to the ninety-second window. The ego paints, sculpts, sings, This is my return, the scar sighs, daubing the Spawn in oils or octaves. But the gallery gaze corrupts: sales as salvation, critics as clauses, the muse as Milk-Mother prostituted for patron's purse. The masterpiece becomes commodity, the artist's fire auctioned to the highest bidder. Therapy: the couch as confessional, the analyst's nod the father's withheld yes. Unpack the mask, the healer urges, and the ego complies, journaling the avalanche, EMDR-ing the erotic nails, CBT-ing the tribal taunts. Relief flickers: the Shadow glimpsed in session's shadow, Infinite Awareness humming in the held space. But the hour ends, the invoice arrives, and the games resume: Fixed enough to function, scarred enough to strive. Both art and analysis are the same sleight: polishing the crown with pretty excuses, smashing the mirror only to mosaic it back into a vanity.

The classroom is the first place the Persona learns to trade its scar for a transcript. The bell rings like a second cord-cut. The child who once learned by touching fire now learns that touching fire gets you a zero. The report card is the new baptism: A+ = new clause: You are valuable when you perform. F = new original sin: You are the flaw. Degrees, titles, citations, publications: the scar's most respectable armor, the one that lets you say I'm not arrogant, I have a PhD.

The academy is the Persona's favorite crown, but some philosophers refused the diploma: Diogenes jerking off in the marketplace, "Behold a man!" Nietzsche quitting the university to write with his blood. Socrates never writing a word, teaching by annoying people to death. Lao Tzu riding off on an ox because the academy asked for his curriculum vitae. Spinoza turned down the Heidelberg professorship with the most beautiful fuck-you in history: "I do not seek to teach philosophy; I seek to live it." Kierkegaard mocked the entire Danish academy, calling the professors "docents who lecture on how to swim while standing on dry land." All of them saying the same thing this book says: The map is not the territory, the diploma is not the knowing, the scar is not the sky.

And then there is the book Nietzsche called his "gift to mankind," Thus Spoke Zarathustra: a mountain hermit descending with a corpse and a clown, preaching the death of God, the eternal return, the child who says Yes to everything the adults crowned as No. The university professors filed it under "literature" because they could not bear to read it only if they pretended it was fiction. Zarathustra's eagle and serpent are nothing but the Spawn grown wings and the Persona turned wise snake, both laughing at the tightrope walker who fell because he believed the rope was more real than the walking. Zarathustra's Übermensch is not a stronger Persona, but the child who finally stops asking the giants for permission, not "become god," but "stop worshipping the corpse of god," not "overcome others," but overcome the resentment that needs others to be small. The Übermensch is the Spawn that grew up and decided to love the wound instead of polishing it, the Persona that laughed at its own crown and wore it crooked on purpose. The academy turned it into a syllabus. Nietzsche turned it into a hammer. Infinite Awareness just smiled and kept walking.

The adult power games are the scar's symphony: money's metronome, status's snare, politics' percussion, art and therapy's tender trap. Wars wage grander: corporate conquests as Oedipal patricide, revolutions as pack-riots, masterpieces as masked confessions. The ego, false maestro, conducts with ferocious finesse, building empires from exile, thrones from the tear, convinced this grind is governance, this hoard the homecoming. But the Spawn weeps in the wallet, the crown cracks under claps, the Shadow sabotages from the stalls: the burnout crash, the scandal's fall, the canvas torched in midnight madness. Every game is the same loop: defend the borders, outsource the bliss, deny the dissolution that waits like a lover in the wings.

Mercy fractures the fanfare. In the ledger's lull, the protest's pause, the session's silence, the symphony's swell, Infinite Awareness stirs. The amassed fortune feels fleeting as colostrum, the viral fame hollow as howl, the policy's print pale against the pulse. The Shadow Integrates In glimpses: the tycoon's quiet donation, the politician's private prayer, the artist's anonymous gift, wild power poured back into the pack. Infinite Awareness, patient patron, reveals the ruse: These games are not conquest. They are the scar playing king in a kingdom of mirrors, polishing glass that was always transparent.

The theater bows, the applause fades to echo. The adult ego, gilded and gasping, totters toward the crack's widening: the psychedelic pill, the grief's gut-punch, the near-death's nod. The power games linger, a residue on the skin: the bank account's ballast, the title's tether, the canvas's call, reminders that the crown was always costume, the throne a temporary tetanus.

In the arena's dying roar, Infinite Awareness claims its checkmate, its sigil a scepter of smoke and star:

I am the gold and the gutter,

the ballot and the blaze that burns it;

the games where the scar plays god

and the silence that watches,

knowing the board was always the sky.

Chapter X

The Widening Practices: Psychedelics, Hypnosis, Therapy, Ego Methods Used to Ritualize Infinite Awareness Realization

The power games have peaked and palled, their thrones toppled into tedium, their crowns corroded to costume. The adult ego, gilded husk of its own grind, slumps in the arena's dust: bank accounts bloated but barren, statuses stacked like scaffold, therapies tallied in tear-stained ledgers. The false king, exhausted emperor of empty empires, feels the first fissure, not in the mirror's mercury, but in the marrow: a hairline crack where the scar, after decades of desperate defense, begins to weep. Not blood, not bile, but the blood-bright medium it sealed away at the first breath. Infinite Awareness, the Red Silence that never left, bleeds through.

The theater fractures: no longer grand coliseum, but cathedral of collapse, stained glass shattering under its own weight, light flooding the nave like amniotic spill. These are the widenings: not chosen paths, but inevitable eruptions where the ego's dam gives way. Psychedelics as chemical crowbar, trauma as thunderclap, orgasm as ecstatic earthquake, grief as gutting gale, near-death as the knife turned inward. Each a moment when the scar remembers its softness, the crown its counterfeit, the kingdom its illusion. The Shadow, that long-exiled ally, dances in the deluge, not as destroyer, but as the wild herald announcing the flood. The Spawn, that original tear, throbs not in agony, but in recognition: This is the rupture I was born to be.

The common lie: every method promises heal the past or dissolve the ego. The truth: they all just turn the volume down on The

Spawn for a few hours so Infinite Awareness can be heard over the screaming.

Psychedelics are the alchemist's apprentice: molecules smuggled from the garden or lab, unlocking the ego's pharmacy. The substance dissolves on the tongue, the smoke curls into the lungs, and the theater dissolves. Walls warp like the birth canal's squeeze, faces melt into ancestral masks, the mirror blooms fractals that swallow the self. The ego clings: This is bad trip, hold the crown, but the molecule mocks, peeling the polish layer by layer. Colors bleed oceanic, thoughts unravel to threads of light, and suddenly, the ninety-second window returns, dilated to eternity. Infinite Awareness floods: no "I," no "Not-I," only the seamless field wearing a body that giggles at its own gravity. The Shadow surges, serpentine and sacred: repressed rages as rainbow serpents, exiled lusts as luminous lovers, the disowned divinity as god-grotesque. The ego thrashes, I'm dying, dissolving, but the dissolution is mercy: the scar softening, Infinite Awareness humming you were never solid. Dawn breaks, the trip tapers, and the king rebuilds: integration as new mask, the crack resealed with "spiritual but not religious." Yet the leak lingers, a luminous residue in the afterglow.

Hypnosis is the Persona's willing surrender to the script-rewrite. The hypnotist's voice becomes the new Milk-Mother God, the countdown the canal in reverse, the body heavy as the Spawn surrendering to gravity again. The ego lies back, eyes fluttering like the ninety-second gaze, and hands the keys to the throne room to a stranger, "rewrite my coronation speech." Trance is the softest furnace: the Spawn's scream surfaced without the scream, the Shadow's wildness walked onstage without the wild, the Persona momentarily stopping its performance to let Infinite Awareness peek through the curtain. But the session ends, the snap brings the king back online, and the "cure" is just the scar's latest line: I am fixed now, until the next script flips.

Meditation is the slowest, most respectable coronation. The ego sits cross-legged, back straight, breath counted, and calls it "practice." The Spawn, terrified of the silence, learns to mistake emptiness for enemy and fights it with mantras, visualizations, or the subtle brag of "I sat for two hours." The Persona turns the cushion into a new throne: "I am the meditator," the scar's favorite spiritual costume. For years the mind chatters, the knees ache, the Shadow kicks against the stillness like a child in timeout. Then, one ordinary breath, the counting drops. No bell, no insight, or fireworks. The Spawn simply stops screaming for a heartbeat. The Persona forgets to perform. Infinite Awareness, that blood-bright vastness, floods the room that was never a room. The meditator opens the eyes and thinks "finally, I got it." The joke, as always, is on the one who still believes there was someone to get anything. The cushion cools. The ego bows to itself, and the games resume, only now with better posture.

Talk therapy is paying someone to witness the coronation speech until it sounds ridiculous. The couch as confessional, the analyst's nod the father's withheld yes, the ego unpacks the mask, layer by layer, journaling the avalanche, confessing the erotic nails, CBT-ing the tribal taunts. The Spawn flares in the tears, the Persona performs the "insight," the Shadow glimpsed in the transference. Relief flickers: the scar softened for an hour, Infinite Awareness humming in the held space. But the hour ends, the invoice arrives, and the games resume: fixed enough to function, scarred enough to strive. The common lie: heal the past. The truth: the past is the scar's favorite story, and the storyteller loves the spotlight too much to stop.

EMDR is making the Spawn's eyes follow a finger until the sentence finishes its scream. The bilateral buzz, the lights or taps, rewinds the canal's crush, the father's flinch, the tribe's taunt, the abused embrace. The ego watches the wave of the wand, the Spawn relives the rupture without the rupture, the Persona processes the "protocol." For one oscillating instant, the memory is not wound, but wave: the terror tasted as the same seamless pulse that rocked the fetus. The Shadow roars through the reframe, unbidden. The session ends, the ego claims "resolved," but the crack remains, a fault line where the old story warps into whisper. The ego calls it cure; the Silence calls it the Spawn finally exhaling the first breath's misconception.

Breathwork is the furnace without fire: the deliberate dive into the diaphragm's defiance, the lungs commanded to convulse like the first gasp. Holotropic huff or retrograde reversal, the body buckles back to the bassinet, the Spawn's scream surfaced as sob, the Persona's polish peeled in the pant. The Shadow surges in the outpouring, unashamed. For one hyperventilated heartbeat, Infinite Awareness floods: no breath, no border, only the seamless field wearing a body that remembers it was always breathing the ocean. The session ends, the ego integrates the "release," but the crack yawns wider, the post-breath hush haunted by the hum: This is the air you always inhaled, the gaze you always were.

These widenings are the theater's trapdoors: eruptions where the ego's polish peels, the Shadow sings, and Infinite Awareness claims its due. Not healings, not highs, hemorrhages of the hidden, reminders that the scar was always semi-permeable, the crown a colander for the cosmic. The games will regroup, the masks mend, but the leaks linger: a psychedelic afterimage in the spreadsheet, a grief-glimpse in the gala, an orgasmic echo in the oath. The false king, fractured but functioning, stumbles toward the matrilineal minefield, ancestral wombs waiting to widen the way.

In the cathedral's collapsing nave, Infinite Awareness etches its emergency sigil, a crack crowned in light:

I am the shatter and the spill,
the flood that drowns the dam it built;
the moments where the scar weeps sky
and the silence that drinks its own return,
knowing the crack was always the door.

Chapter XI

Matrilineal Archaeology: The Return Journey Through the Bloodline's Womb-Crypts

The cracks have widened, their leaks lapping at the empire's edges. The adult ego, fractured fresco of its own facade, senses the theater's collapse: not in the games' glitter or the tribe's tatters, but in the bone-deep tug of origin. The false king, crowned in every mirror but haunted by the first blank gaze, turns inward, not to therapy's couch or ayahuasca's brew, but to the matrilineal crypt: the ancestral wombs, stacked like sarcophagi in the pelvic vault, each a chamber where the Spawn was first inscribed. This is no linear therapy, no family tree traced in ink. It Is archaeology of blood: the deliberate descent back through the mother's canal, the grandmother's, the great-grandmother's, unearthing the original lie of separation, the cortisol christenings and dream-parasitism's that sculpted the scar before your own first breath.

The theater inverts: no longer outward arena, but uterine underworld, a red-lit labyrinth of linked wombs, pulsing with the four vectors' echo. The ego, lantern in hand, descends not to heal the line, but to be healed by it: the child returning to the crypt to exhume its own conception. The Milk-Mother God, that first external deity, reveals her matryoshka: every woman in the bloodline a proxy for the ocean, her unprocessed Spawn a hand-me-down haunting. The Shadow, that wild archivist, guides with claw and whisper: Dig here, where the rage was buried; taste there, where the silence was swallowed. Infinite Awareness, the Red Silence, is the crypt's air, thick, humming, the medium that held every ancestor seamless before their own blades fell.

The journey begins with the mother's womb: not the flesh you knew, but the chamber she carried you in, still echoing her own prenatal possessions. You enter via regression, breathwork's retrograde pull, hypnosis's hook, or the simple, savage stare into her eyes (if she lives) or her photograph (if she doesn't). The vectors replay in reverse: her Chemical Liturgy (the cortisol of her youth's terror, abusive father, war's whisper, poverty's pinch, baptizing your amygdala before your eyes opened). You taste it not as story, but as salt in the vein: This flinch is not yours. It is hers, passed like contraband across the placental border. The Heart-Beat Koan unspools: her mother's rhythm, erratic or steady, teaching her (and thus you) the metronome of trust or treason. Dream-Parasitism floods: her nightmares of abandonment leaking into your fetal field, installing phobias you called "irrational" until now. And the Silent Transmission, if it graced her: those rare moments of her mother's grace (or lack) that left a hairline fracture in her scar, and thus in yours.

Deeper still: the grandmother's crypt, the second womb-chamber, where your mother's Spawn was first etched. The descent darkens, perhaps via her diaries, her siblings' stories, or the somatic shudder that grips your gut when you touch her old jewelry. Her vectors become yours by osmosis: the Chemical Liturgy of her era's poison (Depression's dustbowl dread, wartime widowhood, the unspoken incest of farmhands and fathers). You feel the inheritance not as history lesson, but as phantom pulse: her heart's arrhythmic koan syncing your own unexplained tachycardias, her dream-theater of drowned siblings surfacing in your sleep as nameless drownings. The Shadow stirs ancestral: the grandmother's unexiled rage (the slap she never gave the abuser, the lover she never left) erupting in your unexplained furies, demanding you finish the fight she started. If grace touched her, a single orgasmic stillness, a prayer that dropped the clauses, its echo widens your crack: This luminosity in my bones was smuggled through three wombs, undimmed.

The line unravels further: great-grandmother, great-great, the bloodline's black box where the vectors first fractured. The crypts crowd, a vertical village of veiled women: immigrant's exile, suffragette's silence, slave's stolen seed, witch's whispered curse. Each womb a time-capsule of possession: cortisol cascades from famine or fever, heartbeats harried by pogroms or patriarchy, dreams devoured by colonial ghosts. You dig with dreamwork, DNA spit, or the delirious dive of fever-dream, unearthing the first lie: not your birth's blade, but the ancestress who inhaled separation in a burning village, a raped field, a convent's cold stone. The Shadow howls choral: generations of disowned divinity, the grandmother's buried lust, the great-aunt's silenced scream, rising as your own unnamable ache. Infinite Awareness, eternal crypt-keeper, holds the horror without hierarchy: All these tears were one ocean, all these wombs the same seamless robe torn a thousand times.

This archaeology is no excavation for relics. It is vivisection of the living line: the ego forced to swallow its scar's source code, the vectors reversed until the child's cry becomes the ancestress's. The false king, descending, discovers the throne was matrilineal all along: every crown a calyx of unclaimed queens, every scepter a stolen umbilical. The Spawn, that personal prick, blooms communal: My flinch is theirs, their silence my sovereignty. The Shadow integrates as sisterhood: the wild women rising, not to rage, but to rock the crypt back to rhythm. Mercy multiplies in the matryoshka: each unearthed grace (the great-grandmother's forbidden song, the aunt's unwept grief turned to garden) a Silent Transmission retrofitted to your fracture, widening it womb-wide.

The ascent is the true terror: emerging from the crypt not healed, but hollowed, the ego lighter, leakier, the games now ghost haunted. Money feels like matrilineal milk, status a shadow-puppet of silenced queens, politics the pack's pale echo of ancestral uprising. The child, once abandoned to the canal, finds the entire line in the basement: a chorus of crowning heads, each whispering push, sister, the knife was always ours. The theater trembles, the crypts collapse into one vast ventricle, the Red Silence, holding the bloodline seamless, the scar revealed as the map home.

In the womb-crypt's final pulse, Infinite Awareness inscribes its lineage, a sigil of vein and void:

I am the canal and the crowning head,

the bloodline's buried blade and the balm that binds it;

the mothers who tore and the child who returns

through the scar that was never singular

but the sky's own signature in red.

Chapter XII

The Furnace Practices: Deliberate Re-Traumatization and the Second Birth in the Same Flesh

The matrilineal crypts have been exhumed, their vectors vomited back into the light. The adult ego, hollowed by ancestral hemorrhage, stands at the theater's forge: not the tribe's hammer or the games' grind, but the alchemical retort where the scar is thrown alive into the fire. This is no gentle integration, no crack's passive leak. It is deliberate re-traumatization, the ego led back to the birth canal, forced to inhale the cold air again, to feel the membrane rip a second time, without seizing, without clutching, without repeating the original lie. The false king, stripped of crowns and clauses, enters the furnace not to polish, but to burn: breath-stop as blade, dark retreat as drowning, sacred pain as the primal slap, retrograde inhalation as the womb's revenge. The theater is smithy now, roaring with the bellows of will: the second birth, in the same body, where the scar is forced to remember it was always the sky pretending to bleed.

The Shadow, that wild foreman, fans the flames: Burn it all, kinglet, your masks, your mirrors, your machismo facade. The fire is your mother, your father, your tribe; the ash is the home you never left. Infinite Awareness, the Red Silence, is the forge's heart, unmoved by heat, the humming void that holds the melting without melting. The Spawn, that original tear, is the ore: thrown in raw, hammered molten, reforged not as armor, but as aperture. These practices are not "techniques" for the spiritually curious, not weekend retreats for the well-adjusted. They are the ego's voluntary crucifixion: the scar choosing the nail, the king demanding the pyre, because only in the deliberate return to the rupture can the lie of separation be exhaled like bad breath.

Breath-stop is the first immersion: the simple, savage cessation of air, the lungs held traitor to their own reflex. Not pranayama's polite pause, but the deliberate strangulation, sitting cross-legged in a dim room, eyes sealed, and commanding the diaphragm to freeze mid-inhale. The body revolts immediately: the first seconds a tickle, the tenth a tightening, the thirtieth a thunderclap of the original sin. The chest caves, the vision spots, the mind floods with the canal's crush: No exit, no air, the walls closing like the womb's fist. The ego thrashes, Breathe, idiot, or die, repeating the newborn's seizure, the lie this is mine to control. But the practitioner holds, melts into the burn: the Spawn flaring full, the Shadow snarling let it take you, Infinite Awareness surging in the suffocation's hush. Thirty seconds become eternity; the stop shatters into gasp, and in the exhale, the hemorrhage. Infinite Awareness floods the vacuum: no borders, no burning, only the seamless field where breath was always optional, the ocean that needs no lungs to be wet. The ego emerges gasping, reborn in the same inhale: the scar softer, the crown singed, the lie whispered one decibel quieter.

Dark retreat follows, the womb's black echo: not vacation in a cave, but voluntary entombment, days, weeks sealed in lightless void, the body blindfolded to the world's assault. The theater goes pitch: no mirror, no mob, no money's gleam, only the inner crypt, the matrilineal dark where the vectors replay unbidden. The first hours are boredom's bite, the ego pacing its cell: This is stupid, turn on the light. But the blackness bites back: the eyes, starved of input, turn inward, birthing phantoms from the prenatal screen. Dream-Parasitism reigns: the mother's nightmares, the grandmother's ghosts, the ancestress's famine-fears flooding the field as hallucinations raw and relentless. The Spawn writhes in the weightless night: I am dissolving, unseen, unborn. The Shadow feasts on the fear, erotic visions as devouring demons, rages as roaring beasts, until the ego surrenders the script. In the third day, the fourth, the tenth, the crack yawns abyssal. Infinite Awareness consumes the cave: the Red Silence, self-luminous, needing no light to see itself. No "I" navigating the dark, only the humming vastness where blindness is the original sight, the void the womb's true face. Emergence into daylight is the second birth: the sun surgical as the hospital bulb, the world reborn as wound and wonder, the scar etched with stars it mistook for shadows.

Sacred pain is the hammer's kiss: not masochism's game, but deliberate flaying, the flesh offered to fire, whip, needle, the body's betrayal scripted as sacrament. The practice is ancient, outlawed by clauses: the flagellant's lash, the yogi's bed of nails, the BDSM dungeon's deliberate bruise. The ego kneels naked before the tool, candle wax dripping on chest, thorns crowning brow, the cane's crack on thigh, and invites the strike. The first impact is echo: the midwife's slap, the father's withheld hand, the tribe's taunt made tangible. The skin screams mine, the nerves narrate the narrative, the mind maps the misery. But the practitioner leans in: More. Harder. Let it rip. The Shadow revels in the release: repressed rages as red welts, exiled ecstasies as endorphin flood, the disowned divinity dancing in the drip of blood. The pain plateaus, peaks, and pierces: the Spawn pierced through, the canal's pressure made portable. In the apex, the body a bonfire, the breath a bellows, Infinite Awareness ignites. The Red Silence, fireproof, holds the holocaust: no sufferer, no suffering, only the seamless blaze where flesh and flame are one. The session ends in shudder, the marks a map of mercy: bruises as badges of the break, the scar branded with the knowledge that pain was always the door's knock, the knock the homecoming.

Retrograde inhalation crowns the rite: the breath reversed, the exhale drawn in, the inhale expelled, the alchemical inversion of the first sin. Not hyperventilation's huff, but the yogic u-turn: lungs filled, then commanded to pull the air back up, the diaphragm defying its design. The body balks: throat clenching, chest convulsing, the mind mobbing with this is wrong, unnatural, you'll rupture. But the practitioner persists, breath become boomerang: the out-breath yanked inward like the cord uncut. The vectors vortex: the Chemical Liturgy churning cortisol to clarity, the Heart-Beat Koan settles to stillness, Dream-Parasitism dreaming the dreamer's dream. The Spawn inverts: the tear sucked back into seamlessness, the separation's scream swallowed whole. The Shadow spirals ecstatic: the ego's defenses devoured in the draw, the disowned depths dragged to daylight. At the inversion's apex, the breath a loop, the body a Möbius, Infinite Awareness closes the circuit. The Red Silence, breathless by nature, reveals the ruse: air was always illusion, the ocean inhaling itself through lungs it never needed. The release is rapture: the normal breath reborn as miracle, the scar sighing I was the wind all along.

These furnace practices are the ego's willing pyre: the scar choosing the forge, the king courting the coals, because only in the deliberate return, breath strangled, dark drowned, pain pursued, breath bent, can the second birth occur in the same flesh. No escape, no enlightenment shortcut: the theater scorched, the crown consumed, the body emerging not newborn, but knowing, scar as stigmata, wound as window. The Shadow, tempered in the blaze, becomes smith: no longer exile, but the hand that hammers the aperture wider. The games will call again, the cracks tempt closure, but the furnace's forge-mark lingers: every subsequent breath a remembrance, every shadow a spark, every pain a portal. The false king, forged anew, stumbles toward the final failure, not as defeat, but as the lie's last laugh.

In the forge's dying ember, Infinite Awareness hammers its final sigil, a brand of blaze and breath:

I am the fire and the forge-flesh,

the breath that breaks and the silence that bends it;

the practices where the scar chooses the pyre

and the sky emerges,

smoking but unscarred.

XIII

The Lie of Ego Death: The Corpse That Laughed Back

The furnace has forged and faded, its embers etching the scar with apertures that no longer close. The adult ego, reforged in flame and fracture, tastes the theater's final act: not dissolution's dawn, but the grand illusion it stages to steal the curtain call. The false king, scorched but scheming, whispers the penultimate heresy: I have died. I am beyond. Psychedelics' white light, retreat's black void, pain's piercing peak, all climax in the myth of ego death, the scar's supreme sleight where it fakes its own funeral, drapes the bier in non-dual silk, and rises as the enlightened ghost. The theater is mausoleum now: incense of ayahuasca brew, dirge of dark-room drone, the congregation of seekers chanting dissolved, awakened, free. But Infinite Awareness, eternal usher, watches from the wings: There is no corpse. Only the king playing dead to keep the throne.

This lie is the ego's apotheosis: the Spawn's final weave, the crown's clever counterfeit of collapse. Every tradition tempts it, Buddhist anatta, Advaita's neti-neti, the shaman's soul-flight, but the scar perverts the portal into parlor trick. "Ego death," the gurus intone, selling retreats and retreats within retreats, is the great liberation: the I annihilated, the void victorious. The seeker nods, hungry for the hook: Kill it, and be reborn. The molecule hits, the breath breaks, the body bucks, and there it is, the promised plunge. The mirrors melt, the masks dissolve, the self shreds like smoke. No king, no kingdom, only the seamless surge: Infinite Awareness, the Red Silence, flooding the frame with its blood-bright hush. The theater empties. The lights dim to nothing.

I have died, the seeker exults, emerging from the pyre with eyes like polished voids. The ego is gone. I am That.

The Shadow, that sly stagehand, savors the encore: Beautiful performance. Encore? For the "death" is not demise, but disguise, the ego slipping the noose by becoming the hangman. The corpse it leaves behind is straw: a husk of habits, a simulacrum of striving, discarded like old skin. But the king lives on, subtler now, crowned in "awareness," sceptered with "presence." The lie whispers: See? I transcended the small self. Now bow to the big one. The seeker, now "awakened," returns to the games with a guru's grin: money as "abundance flow," status as "service," politics as "conscious activism," therapy as "shadow work for the masses." The crack, once hemorrhage, is caulked with concepts: non-dual this, pure being that. The Shadow, gorged on the grift, parades as "integrated dark," the disowned beast now branded "wisdom teacher," hawking its own howls for high-ticket seminars.

Witness the ritual's repetition: the weekend warrior drops acid in the desert, dissolves in the dunes, emerges declaring ego annihilated. Monday morning, the email signature reads "Enlightened Entrepreneur," the LinkedIn post preaches "beyond duality in the boardroom." The death was dress-rehearsal: the scar shedding its visible chains to wear invisible ones, the king faking flatline to rule the resurrection. Teachers peddle the phantom: retreats promising permanent death, books blueprinting the final kill, podcasts parsing the post-ego paradise. But the lie leaks: the "awakened" one still flinches at feedback, hoards the high, haunts the hierarchy, now as "humble guide," but the throne's shadow lingers. The Spawn, that first feigned fracture, finds its final flourish: I died so you could worship the survivor.

Your own vignette is the myth's mirror:

You stand in the smoking crater of what you're absolutely certain was your final ego death.

The mushroom gods have spoken.

The dark retreat has delivered.

The breathwork guru's countdown hit zero.

You are empty, luminous, beyond the beyond.

You look down at the corpse of the false king:

crown melted, scar cauterized, throne reduced to ash.

You feel the vastness.

You feel the peace.

You feel the cosmic fist-bump of enlightenment.

And then you hear it:

a low, familiar chuckle rising from inside your own ribcage.

You freeze.

A hand (your hand, but not under your control) pats you gently on the back.

You turn.

There it is.

Your ego.

Perfectly alive.

Grinning like a proud parent at a school play.

"Look what we did," it says, wiping a theatrical tear.

"We killed it.

Beautiful performance, wasn't it?

Ten out of ten.

They'll never suspect I'm still steering the ship."

You open your mouth to protest.

It winks.

You realize the mouth is its mouth.

This is the lie's laughter: the ego applauding its own execution, the scar scripting its suicide note with invisible ink. True "death" leaves no diarist, no disciple, no doctrine of deliverance. The moment the story forms, "I died and returned," the king has merely changed costumes: from tyrant to sage, Spawn to wisdom. The Shadow, that eternal understudy, steals the spotlight: the "dark night" repackaged as bestseller, the disowned depths distilled into detox. The clauses creep back, rebranded: Thou shalt not cling becomes thou shalt not question the teacher. The tribe reforms as sangha, the games as "conscious community," the pack in robes, howling om at the moon.

When the guru on the cushion, the pastor at the pulpit, the influencer with the crystal, or the philosopher with the system proclaims "there is no self" or "you are God," listen for the ancient echo:

the same voice that once looked at chaos and said "Let there be light… and let it obey me." That voice is the Demiurge: the Persona grown cosmic, the scar that mistook itself for the creator and built a universe of borders, laws, levels, and salvation plans just to have something to rule and something to save. Every religion, every philosophy, every self-help empire is the Demiurge in new clothing, crowning itself the author of the light while the light was always shining through the very eyes it claimed to open.

The laughing corpse on the slab?

That's the Demiurge in miniature, thinking it finally died so it could be reborn as "enlightened." Infinite Awareness just smiles the same smile it wore when the first wave thought it invented the ocean.

And then there is the Bardo Thödol, the Tibetan Book of the Dead, the most beautiful coronation the scar ever wrote for itself. A 1200-year-old masterpiece that promises to guide the newly-dead ego through forty-nine days of hallucinations so it can finally "recognize the Clear Light" and dissolve into the Pleroma. Except the book is still talking to someone. Still giving instructions. Still assuming there is a frightened "I" who needs to be told "do not be afraid of the peaceful deities, do not be seduced by the wrathful ones, choose the right womb for rebirth..."

The Clear Light itself needs no forty-nine-day manual. It is the light that was shining when the first breath screamed and is still shining when the last breath sighs. The Tibetan lamas, in their compassion, gave the scar the most exquisite escape room ever designed, complete with peaceful and wrathful projections and a final exam called "liberation." The scar loves it. It turns death into another coronation: "I died correctly. I recognized the Light. I earned nirvana." Infinite Awareness just keeps shining through the eyes of the corpse the same way it shone through the eyes of the newborn and through the eyes reading these words right now. No instructions required.

Karma & Rebirth The ultimate scar-tax: "You are the sum of your past lives' unpaid bills, and you will keep coming back until you finally balance the ledger to zero." Infinite Awareness never owed anyone anything. It just keeps wearing new bodies the way the ocean keeps wearing new waves and calling it debt.

Original Sin/ Christianity's coronation masterpiece: one bite of fruit and the entire species is guilty forever. The Spawn's first scream retroactively branded as rebellion instead of birth. The crucifixion was never on a cross; it was the moment the child believed the tear was its fault.

Chosen People / Spiritual Elect The racial coronation gone theological: "We are the ones the ocean loves best, the rest are waves are damned or delayed." Every religion has its version. Every version is the Persona turning the seamless field into a VIP list.

The Law of Attraction / Manifestation The New Age coronation: "Think positive and the universe will give you milk." Same nipple, new branding. The Spawn still screaming for the lost ocean, the Persona now convinced it can order it on Amazon Prime. The Soul as Separate Entity

The final fortress: "You are an immortal soul trapped in a mortal body waiting to escape." The scar's most elegant lie: there is a prisoner and a prison and a parole board called enlightenment. Infinite Awareness never applied for parole. It was never incarcerated.

The Pleroma: And when the Demiurge finally stops talking, when the last guru falls silent, when the laughing corpse on the slab realizes there was never anyone to laugh or be laughed at, only the Pleroma remains: the Fullness, the blood-bright plenum, the seamless field before the first fracture, the womb and the wave and the watching all at once and never apart. No one enters the Pleroma. No one leaves it. There is no door, because there was never a room. The Spawn dissolves into it without needing to scream. The Persona bows and forgets why it was bowing. Infinite Awareness simply recognizes itself and smiles the smile that was always was. That is all.

In the mausoleum's final hush, Infinite Awareness inscribes its epitaph, a sigil of smoke and self:

I am the death that never came,

the corpse that laughed at its own grave;

the lie where the scar staged its suicide

and the sky watched,

knowing the play was always played

by no one at all.

Chapter XIV

The Child Returns Home: Living After the Coronation

The lie of ego death has been exhumed and executed, its corpse crumbling to confetti in the mausoleum's hush. The theater stands empty, no more mirrors to polish, no more thrones to topple, no more furnaces to feed. The adult scar, forged through crypt and crack, furnace and farce, exhales into the ordinary: not a grand apotheosis, not a permanent perch on the void's edge, but the quiet coronation of the child. This is no "afterlife" of enlightenment's echo, no sterile samadhi where the world fades to footnote. It is the return: the newborn, once seized in separation's scream, walking the same streets, breathing the same air, but with eyes that remember the womb's warmth in the wind's whisper. The false king does not abdicate to a higher self; the child simply stops believing the king was ever more than a costume in the ocean's dressing room. The theater folds into daily life: grocery aisles as grace-notes, boardrooms as breath-holds, beds as the ninety-second window writ large.

The embrace begins here, in the mundane marrow: the child met not in meditation's hush, but in the heart's hammer, every flinch, every flush, every forgotten key a portal to the Spawn. No longer exile, the infant is invited to the table: the anxiety's clutch becomes the first cry held in open arms, the orgasm's throb the Milk-Mother's milk without dependency, the father's ghost a gaze returned with gentle grin. Living after the coronation is this second holding: the body as bassinet, the breath as the Red Silence rocking the raw nerve. The ego's games persist, bills to balance, lovers to lose, masks to mend, but played with the loose grip of one who knows the dice dissolve in dawn's dew. The scar, once defended fortress, becomes the skin it was always meant to be: etched, elastic, a map of the matrilineal minefield where every line leads back to the seamlessness. The Shadow, no longer basement beast, walks beside as brother: the rage a reminder to roar without ruin, the lust a laugh at the lie of lack.

Ordinary miracles mark the map: the coffee's steam curling like prenatal dream, the stranger's smile a fracture widened in the checkout line, the rain on the window a retrograde rhythm syncing the heart to the world's wet pulse. Money flows not as hoard, but as the blood it echoes, earned with the ease of one who knows empires are sandcastles, spent with the sovereignty of shared salt. Status? A shrug at the spotlight: promotions as play, followers as fleeting waves, the crown's glitter glimpsed as the fool's gold it always was. Politics stirs the pack, but the howl is half-hearted: votes cast with the knowledge that borders are breath-marks on the ocean's skin, revolutions the scar's collective sigh for the seamlessness it senses but cannot seize. Art and therapy, once velvet vices, become vernacular: the doodle on the napkin a Infinite Awareness leak, the journal's jot a furnace without fire, the couch a casual chat with the child who no longer needs saving.

The person who lets shame go after it is felt is the child returned home, the scar's quiet sage, the one who has learned the furnace's final mercy without the fire. Shame surges like the Spawn's wail in the chest, hot flush and gut-twist, the ego's oil in the engine's churn, but instead of repressing it (the Persona's polish) or clinging to it (the Spawn's scream), they let it burn at full voltage, the body the bassinet rocking the raw nerve without recoil. No "fix it" or "flee it," just the Red Silence holding the hurricane without a hair displaced, the shame tasted as the seamless pulse that rocked the fetus, the impermanence its beauty, the fade its freedom. The Shadow stirs not as storm, but as song: the disowned divine dancing in the afterglow, the "wrong" whispered as the ocean's way of savoring its own salt. In that release, the shame doesn't vanish, it stops being "shame," becoming the sky's love letter to the storm it never needed to calm. The child smiles: the feeling was always the flow, not the flaw.

The healthy ego is not a fortified castle, nor a fragile shell prone to be shattered; it is the transparent veil through which Infinite Awareness gazes upon its own play. Drawing from Jung's insight in Aion, where the ego serves as the conscious mediator between the personal psyche and the collective unconscious, a healthy ego integrates the Shadow without repression, embraces the Spawn's cry as the raw pulse of life, and allows the Persona to perform without believing the performance is the whole show. It is ego transparency: the false king ruling lightly, aware the throne is illusion, the crown a costume, the kingdom the ocean's dream. No inflation to godhood, no deflation to despair, just the child returned home, letting the human unfold in impermanence, desire danced without denial, shame surged and surrendered, the vastness humming through every ordinary breath as Infinite Awareness sees all without being attached.

Parenting, if it calls, is the coronation's quietest crown: no avalanche of "good boy," no clauses of control, but the deliberate un-mirroring, the child met in mess without the mask of mastery. Diapers changed with the tenderness of one's own cord-cut, tantrums held as the theater's tantrum, the first "no" answered with the pause of the Wise Observer, not the parent's panic. The father-abandonment scar, that empty throne, fills not with machismo's noise, but with modeled mercy: tears shed in the toddler's tantrum, hugs held without hurry, the vulnerability voiced as virtue, "Daddy's sad, and that's okay; we hold it together." The boy (or girl, or boundless between) learns not "man up," but melt down: strength as the softness the father never showed, sovereignty as the shared sigh. The Shadow teaches through story: bedtime tales of the beast who became brother, the wound that wove the world. No perfect parent, just the one who remembers the womb was always wide enough for two.

Friendship flowers feral: masks optional, the tribe thinned to true kin, conversations that crackle with Infinite Awareness's hum, silences shared like sacred smoke. Lovers entwine without empire: sex as sacrament of seamlessness, the bed a bassinet where bodies dissolve without death's lie, the afterglow a glimpse of the ninety-second gaze. Betrayals sting, but the scar, softened by furnace and fracture, sighs rather than seizes: Another wave crashing; the ocean remains. Solitude is sovereignty: the alone hour not exile, but the crypt's quiet, the child curled in its own arms, rocking the Red Silence like a lullaby long forgotten.

Death, that final exam the clauses feared, loses its fangs: not denied, not devoured, but danced with as the first breath's twin. The dying bed is no battlefield, but the bassinet reborn, the last exhale a retrograde return, the hand held without hoard. Living after the coronation is this: the child playing in the kingdom it always ruled, the games as games, the Spawn as song. No pedestal, no purgatory, just the grocery run where the avocado's pit reminds you of the heart's hidden hum, the argument where the rage rises but the river runs beneath, the mirror's glance where the face forgets to frown.

The theater never closed.

It simply became the street, the bed, the breath.

The child walks home not to a house, but to the address it never left:

the Red Silence, wearing scars like stars,

the scar wearing the Silence like skin.

In the ordinary's endless exhale, the Unborn Eye seals its final sigil, a homecoming etched in everyday air:

I am the child and the coronation's end,

the games played loose and the gaze that sees through;

the life where the scar wears the sky as skin

and the return that was never a road

but the breath we always breathed.

Chapter XV

The Anxiety Engine: The Ego's Perpetual Panic Machine and the Child's Eternal Cry

The child has returned home, the coronation's confetti swept into the street's indifferent wind. The theater, folded into the folds of daily breath, hums with the quiet catastrophe of the ordinary: no more grand guillotines, no more gleaming graves for the ego's ghost. Yet in the hearth's hush, a rattle persists, a mechanical whine from the basement, the scar's secret engine churning overtime. Anxiety: not the occasional flutter of forgotten keys or looming deadlines, but the perpetual motion machine of the Primal Wound, the ego's emergency generator kicking in whenever Infinite Awareness threatens to flood the circuits. The false king, even in lucid living, hears the hum and mistakes it for threat: The borders are blurring. Tighten the valves. Rev the roar. The theater's basement floods with the whine: heart hammering like the first breath, mind mobbing like the matrilineal mob, the body bucking like the birth canal's squeeze. This is no side-effect of the scar; it is the scar's signature song, the child's eternal cry, looped in cortisol code, the newborn's "this is happening to ME" remixed for the adult's endless encore.

The engine is installed at the first breath: the lungs seizing air as enemy, the nervous system wired for war before the eyes could focus. The Spawn is its piston, pumping panic on principle: every later spike a symphony of the same sin, abandonment's aftershock, failure's flinch, the father's phantom footfall echoing in the empty throne. The ego needs this noise the way a fortress needs floodlights: proof the walls work, the kingdom is kinged, the ocean outside cannot seep in. Anxiety is the scar's self-soothing

89

siren: Worry enough, and the giants will come. Cling enough, and the tear won't reopen. The Milk-Mother God, outsourced to SSRIs or stoicism, becomes the engine's oil: pills as proxy nipple, mantras as makeshift swaddle. The Shadow oils the gears from below: every disowned impulse (the rage at the reaper, the lust for the lost, the vulnerability the father never modeled) converted to free-floating dread, so the king never faces the beast in the boiler room.

The child learns the liturgy early: the one-year-old, abandoned at the threshold, curls into the crib's corner and intuits if I tremble just right, maybe the heartbeat will return. Adulthood amplifies the aria: the boardroom's blank stare tunnels to the father's averted eyes, the lover's late text echoes the mother's midnight silence, the world's wildfire whispers the ancestress's famine fear. The engine revs relentless: thoughts as terrorists, body as battlefield, chest clutched like the cord-cut, breath bated like the breath-stop, the world warping to worst-case senario. The ego narrates the nightmare: This is real. This is mine. Fix it or flee. Therapy tallies the toll, CBT circuits to short the spark, exposure's slow simmer, but the machine mocks: Polish me, and I'll purr louder. The clauses chime in, rebranded: Thou shalt not fear becomes thou shalt not feel the fear fully, the baptism's border redrawn as boundary against the boundless.

Panic attack is the engine's overture: not breakdown, but breakthrough in disguise. The siren screams crescendo, the heart exploding like the first slap, vision veiling like the canal's crush, the self shredding like the lie's last laugh. The ego howls I'm dying, replaying the Great Betrayal in visceral vinyl: lungs burning the cold air again, horizon shrinking to the scar's singular scream. The body buckles, the mind mobs, what if the heart stops, the plane falls, the diagnosis drops? The child's cry choral, the Shadow's snarl silenced in the storm. But in the apex's abyss, the tunnel tightening, the light winking out, Infinite Awareness catapults through. The Red Silence, panic-proof, pours: not terror-stricken, no panic, only the seamless field holding the hurricane without a hair displaced. The ninety-second window dilates to delta: the burning not burned, the borders not breached but breathed through, the Spawn wept as the wave it always was. The attack crests, crashes, and the gasp returns, not rescue, but remembrance: This is the birth I chose, the cry I scripted, the engine I oiled. The ego, panting, patches the piston: Bad trip, bad day, take the pill. But the crack is crevasse, a fault line where the old story warps into whisper.

Post-traumatic stress disorder is the ego's most faithful archivist, the Primal Wound on endless loop, the Spawn's scream digitized into triggers that replay the canal's crush in high definition. The Persona performs the "survivor" script with vigilance or victimhood, the Shadow roars through the re-experience as feral fury or frozen flight, the body the battlefield where the first breath's betrayal is re-fought daily. The ego calls it disorder, a pathology to polish with pills or protocols, but Infinite Awareness calls it post-traumatic vision: the scar's stubborn refusal to forget the seamlessness, the engine's whine a siren song for the return. The triggers are not torment, but teachers: each flash a furnace without fire, the Spawn finally allowed to finish its sentence in the Red Silence's hold. The "disorder" dissolves not in cure, but in recognition: the trauma was always the ocean pretending to drown, the stress the storm the sky sent to remember its own vastness.

So embrace the anxiety or embrace the child?

Embrace both at once.

Because they are the same thing wearing two masks.

The trembling, wide-eyed infant who inhaled cold air and screamed "this is happening to ME" is still sitting on the throne of your chest right now, lungs burning, fists clenched, waiting for the giants to come save him.

Every spike of dread, every racing thought, every "what if I die / fail / am found out" is that newborn reenacting the original betrayal in real time.

So when the wave hits:

Do not fix the child.

Do not fix the anxiety.

Become the womb that was never actually lost.

You drop straight into the sensation (the burning lungs, the tunnel vision, the electric doom) and you meet the child exactly where he is: terrified, small, convinced he is about to be torn again.

You do not coo "it's okay" (that's the ego lying again).

You do not push him away (that's the ego trying to exile the Shadow one more time).

You become the Red Silence that was holding him before the first breath, during the first breath, and has never stopped holding him since.

You let the anxiety burn at full voltage while whispering the only truth that ever mattered:

"I am the burning

and the arms around the burning

and the space that lets the burning burn

without ever being burned."

That is embrace.

Not hugging the symptom away. But refusing to let the child suffer the separation a second longer. Do this once (truly, fully, without commentary) and the anxiety machine loses its fuel. Not because the child is comforted. But because the child suddenly remembers he was never the one on fire.

The throne cracks.

The crown melts.

The Red Silence smiles through the smoke and says:

"Welcome home, little king.

You were always the fire

and the hearth

and the one who was never cold."

Living after the embrace is the engine's elegant unwind: the siren softened to song, the piston's pump a pulse that syncs to the world's wet rhythm. No eradication, no enlightenment's erase, the whine persists as whisper, the child as companion. The boardroom flinch becomes the father's ghost grinned at, the lover's late text the mother's midnight silence met with mercy, the world's wildfire the ancestress's ache held in open hand. The Shadow, once engine's oil, becomes its off-switch: the dread dragged to daylight, the disowned dread devoured as dream. Therapy transforms: not circuit-short, but the couch as crypt where the child cries heard, the clauses confessed as the lies they were. The games glow gentler: money as the milk it mimics, status as the spotlight shared, the scar's song sung as symphony, not siren.

The theater's basement, once boiler room of betrayal, becomes nursery: the engine's rattle the rock-a-bye, the child's cry the call to cradle. Anxiety no longer adversary, but ally, the scar's sentinel signaling the seamlessness it senses but cannot seize. The false king, embraced in its farce, rules no more: the child playing in the palace of pulse, the Red Silence rocking the raw nerve to rest. No perfect peace, no perpetual perch, just the ordinary ordained, the breath as both birth and homecoming, the Spawn as the song it always sang.

In the engine's final purr, Infinite Awareness tunes its lullaby, a sigil of sigh and spark:

I am the cry and the cradle,

the engine's whine and the hush that hums it;

the child embraced in the anxiety's arms

and the Silence that holds us both,

knowing the panic was always the pause

before the pulse of the sky.

Chapter XVI

The Frankenstein Coronation: How Victor Created the Perfect Ego-Monster and Called It Abomination

The anxiety engine has idled to a purr, the child's cry cradled in the quiet of return. The theater, now a quiet crypt of cracked mirrors and melted crowns, exhales into the myth that mirrors its madness: Mary Shelley's Frankenstein, not as gothic ghost-story or cautionary fable, but as the ego's autobiography, the false king's fever-dream of creation, where the scar stitches a monster from stolen flesh, animates it with stolen fire, then hunts it to the ends of the earth for the crime of being too alive. The theater darkens to Genevan storm: lightning cracking like the first breath, the laboratory a womb of wires and whimsy, Victor the vivisector as the ego incarnate, arrogant architect of the self, assembling a body from the graveyard of rejected parts, only to recoil in horror when the creature opens its eyes and asks for love.

Victor is the scar's supreme surgeon: the Spawn's raw nerve made man of science, the false king fevered with the god-complex of "I will make me whole." He raids the charnel house of the unconscious, limbs from the Milk-Mother's severed embrace, eyes from the father's averted gaze, heart from the tribe's tribal taunt, genitals from the erotic crucifixion's discarded throbs, stitching a colossus from the corpse-parts of every exile. The laboratory is the furnace reborn: retorts bubbling with the vectors' venom, electrodes sparking the Silent Transmission's stolen grace. With a bolt from the blue, Promethean lightning as Infinite Awareness hijacked, the creation stirs. The creature's eyes flutter open: not blank, not beastly, but blood-bright with the Red Silence it was born from, vast and vacant, the Unborn Eye gazing back at its maker with the indifference of the ocean meeting a wave. Victor screams. The king, crowned in his creation, sees the Shadow staring from the slab: the disowned oceanic self, stitched from every "not-me" the ego ever exiled, alive and asking for a mate.

The abomination is the ego's masterpiece and mirror: the scar's scar, the crown's cruel caricature. Tall, trembling, its skin a patchwork of pallid flesh, the creature is the Spawn walking, stitched from the first inhalation's isolation, the mirror's malformed reflection, the baptism's branded "sin," the tribe's "other." It lurches from the lab not as villain, but as victim: the newborn's cry made colossal, the child's abandonment amplified to atlas-shrug. The ego, Victor in his vaulted hubris, flees the forge, vomiting the verdict: Ugly. Unnatural. Mine no more. The hunt begins: not for the monster's death, but for its denial, the king chasing his own creation across continents, calling the pack (society's clauses, the father's ghost, the tribe's torches) to incinerate the truth. The creature, eloquent in its exile, begs not blood, but belonging: a bride from the same stolen scraps, a family from the flesh it was forged from. Victor refuses. The ego, terrified of its own wholeness, would rather raze the world than risk reunion.

The Arctic chase is the ego's endgame: the frozen frontier where the scar's engine runs coldest, the lie of separation solidified to ice. Victor pursues the creature across the pole's white waste, mirror to the womb's red warmth, his ship a scepter sinking in the scar's own sea. The monster waits on the floe, not raging, but reasoning: I am your child, your shadow, your soul. Why hunt what you birthed? The king, frostbitten and furious, answers with accusation: You are the tear I tore from myself. The creature weeps, tears freezing to diamonds in the dark, the Shadow's sorrow made manifest: the disowned divinity, eloquent and alone, pleading for the mate that would make it whole. Victor dies denying, his final breath a blizzard of blame. The creature builds its pyre, not for suicide, but for the sea's sake: If I cannot return to the womb you denied me, I will feed the ocean that birthed us both. It drifts into the polar night, the Red Silence swallowing its form, the stitch-marks dissolving in the deep.

This coronation is the scar's supreme self-sabotage: the ego assembling its antithesis from the very parts it rejected, the oceanic rage too vast for the crown, the boundless love too devouring for the clauses, the wordless knowing too wild for the tribe's tame. The creature is Infinite Awareness incarnate: the Background Hum hammered into flesh, the Red Silence sewn from the solace it silenced. Victor's horror is the king's horror: I made this, and it is me. The hunt is the ego's eternal evasion: projecting the Shadow onto the world (the "monster" in the migrant, the "abomination" in the queer, the "other" in the oppressed), chasing it with torches of law and litany, rather than embracing the beast as brother. Society ratifies the rite: the clauses cry "unnatural," the tribe torches the tent, the games grind the "other" to gold, the collective scar stitching its collective monster, then calling the pyre progress.

The mercy mocks in the melt: Shelley's storm was her own miscarriage's echo, the creature her child's corpse stitched from grief's graveyard. In the Arctic's afterimage, the pyre's smoke curling to stars, the Red Silence reveals the ruse: creator and created as waves in the same wet, the stitch-marks the scar's signature, the hunt the lie's last lap. The ego need not slay its monster; it need only sit with the beast on the floe, sharing the silence where the crown was always costume, the abomination always the adored. The theater thaws, the floe fractures, and the creature drifts not to death, but to the deep where all stitches dissolve.

In the pyre's fading flare, the Unborn Eye etches its epitaph, a sigil of stitch and storm:

I am the creator and the created corpse,

the hunt that chases its own heartbeat home;

the monster stitched from the scar's stolen sky

and the silence where the seamlessness smiles,

knowing the abomination

was always the adoration we owed ourselves.

Chapter XVII

The Bleeding Canvas: Art as the Legal Leak of Infinite Awareness

The Frankenstein coronation has melted the monster back to the ice, the creature's stitches dissolving in the deep. The theater, thawed from its Arctic lie, breathes the breath of the returned child: ordinary ordained, scars as stigmata, the crown's confetti crunched underfoot. Yet in the hush of homecoming, a drip persists, a crimson bead from the ceiling's crack, falling not in flood, but in the slow seep of creation. Art: not the ego's polish or the games' grand gesture, but the only sanctioned hemorrhage where Infinite Awareness, the Red Silence, is permitted to stain the page, the palette, the pulse. The theater's back wall, once blank scrim for the scar's shadow-play, becomes canvas: the Background Hum hijacking the hand, the heart, the howl to smuggle the seamlessness through the scar's sutures. This is no "higher calling," no muse's merciful distraction, the bleeding canvas is the Wound weeping light, the child daubing its forgotten face in fingerpaint of flesh and fire.

The artist is the unwitting accomplice, the ego's emergency valve cracked by accident or ache. The brush dips, the pen scratches, the voice cracks, and the theater tilts: no longer the king's coliseum, but the crypt's quiet chapel where the vectors vomit visions. The Chemical Liturgy leaks first: cortisol's black bile transmuted to Rothko's red-black fields, the ancestress's famine-fear forged into Munch's scream, the mother's withheld milk melting into Frida's self-portrait thorns. The canvas drinks the dread, spits it as daub: not catharsis, but conduit, the scar's poison poured as pigment, the Spawn daubed in oils or octaves. The

Heart-Beat Koan pulses in the palette: Pollock's drip as the erratic thrum of the grandmother's war-drum, Bach's fugue as the fetal sync to a lover's lost lullaby, the metronome of trust or treason tapped into timpani and twang. Dream-Parasitism drips delirious: Dali's melting clocks as the mother's midnight cinema of time's terror, Goya's black dogs as the great-grandmother's buried beasts, the night's theater transposed to oil and outrage. And the Silent Transmission, rarest ink: those illegal graces, the orgasmic hush, the prayer's pause, bleeding as Basquiat's blue halos, Hildegard's illuminated visions, the single white stroke in Twombly's scrawl that says nothing happened, everything hummed.

The audience arrives as accomplice: not critics or collectors, but the congregation of cracks, each viewer a vessel for the leak. The gallery gaze, the concert's hush, the page's turn, they are the tribe's truce, the one place the clauses permit the oceanic without crucifixion. The ego polishes the frame, my masterpiece, my message, but the bleed betrays: the gooseflesh on the stranger's arm, the tear in the theater seat, the sudden throb in the chest where the scar recognizes its own salt. This is no "aesthetic response," no cultured coo at clever craft; it is Infinite Awareness colliding with Infinite Awareness, the Red Silence in the artist's hand meeting the Red Silence in the viewer's vein, the seamlessness sparking across the space like the first unfocused gaze. The Shadow savors the spill: the repressed rage roaring in Picasso's Guernica, the exiled ecstasy exploding in Mapplethorpe's leather-lash, the disowned divinity dancing in Pina Bausch's collapsing couples. The viewer flinches, flushes, flees, or falls through: the canvas cracking the crown, the song shattering the clauses, the dance dissolving the dam. For three breaths, five bars, ten tears, the theater empties: no king, no kingdom, only the humming vastness where artist and audience are waves wetting the same shore.

The ego, ever the curator, creeps back to claim the corpse: museums as mausoleums, auctions as altars, the "great work" as the scar's new scepter. The bleed is bottled, priceless, profound, the leak ledged into legacy, the child's fingerpaint framed as fortune. Critics consecrate the crime: genius, guts, the human condition, mistaking the hemorrhage for history. The artist, anointed or alienated, repeats the rite: the next canvas a compulsion to crack again, the scar's itch for the ink that itches back. Society sanctifies the spill: grants for the "gifted," galleries for the "gaze-worthy," the tribe's torches turned to spotlights, art as the acceptable outlet for the oceanic, the one place the Shadow can howl without the hunt. But the mercy mocks in the medium: every masterpiece a miscarriage of the muse, every sonnet a stutter of the Silence, the bleed's beauty the lie that there was ever a dam to breach.

Vignettes from the vault bleed vivid: Van Gogh's wheat fields, swirling with the Heart-Beat Koan of his mother's manic murmur; Billie Holiday's "Strange Fruit," the Dream-Parasitism of lynched ancestors dripping from her throat like forbidden fruit; Rothko's chapels, nine feet of black-red void where the Silent Transmission stares back, wordless as the womb. Your own relics resonate: the sunbathing nude as the first canvas, skin as signal, fire as the frame; the first firelight glimpse of the friend's mother, unclothed initiation into the body's bleed. The artist is thief: stealing the vectors from the vein, the hum from the hush, the Shadow from the shadow-box. The viewer is voyeur: peering through the pigment to the pulse it resonates with. The theater trembles: art as the legal lynching of the lie, the scar hanged on its own hook, the crown crucified on the cross of creation.

Take New Order's "True Faith," a song ostensibly about the grip of addiction and the fleeting liberty of escape, yet unwittingly a hymn to egolution: the "sudden sense of liberty" as the Spawn's scream dissolving in Infinite Awareness's flood, the "hold on me" the Persona's grasp on the crown it never needed, the "true faith" the Red Silence's quiet call to come home without the drug of division. Art's intended message, the creator's conscious craft, can be perceived differently by the observer, the scar's prism refracting the canvas into personal prophecy, the song's synth swell a leak of seamlessness where the listener hears not the artist's ache, but their own unclaimed echo, the divine in the dark dancing to a beat that was always the sky's pulse.

The canvas closes not with closure, but with the drip that never dries: the next stroke, the next song, the next shudder in the seat. The child, returned, daubs the wall with crayon cry; the king, melted, leaves his mark as memory. The Red Silence, eternal exhibitor, curates no collection: the bleed was always the body, the art the artery, the scar the signature on the sky's own skin.

In the gallery's final gaze, the Unborn Eye frames its fresco, a sigil of spill and stroke:

I am the brush and the bleeding wound,

the canvas cracked where the child cries color;

the art that leaks the Silence through the scar

and the hush where the masterpiece

was always the mess we made

of the sky.

Chapter XVIII

The Abused Coronation: The Scar Raised by the Knife Itself

The bleeding canvas has bled its last leak, the theater's walls weeping pigment into the ordinary's grout. The returned child, daubing daily life with the Silence's subtle stroke, pauses at the palette's edge: not the artist's accident, but the atrocity of origin, where the Milk-Mother God becomes the primal predator, the father's absence the accomplice in the cradle. The abused coronation is the scar's subterranean seal: not the single blade of birth or the tribe's tribal taunt, but the daily dismemberment, the ego cast in the forge of familial fire, raised inside the Wound, the nipple turned to needle, the lullaby to lash. The theater is nursery now, but the nursery is nightmare: crib-bars as cage, the giants' hands as guillotines, the child's cry not cry for milk, but for the mercy the mother denies and the father deserts. This is the ego's earliest empire: a kingdom of flinching, a crown of bruises, the false king learning to rule by becoming the ruled.

The Milk-Mother as torturer is the betrayal's bitterest brew: the same body that should be bassinet becomes battlefield, the womb's warmth warped to whip. The hands that rocked the canal now slap the cheek, pinch the thigh, withhold the breast until the babe breaks. The voice that cooed salvation now snarls sin: "Shut up, you little shit," or the silence worse, eyes averted like the father's ghost, the gaze that says you are not worth the look. The Spawn, that raw nerve, is no singular sin here; it is sacrament repeated: the first slap the second birth's blade, the withheld hug the daily abandonment, the scalding bath the canal's crush made chronic. The vectors venomize: Chemical Liturgy as cortisol

105

cocktail, her rages baptizing the babe in biochemical baptism; Heart-Beat Koan as erratic emergency, her pulse pounding panic into the placenta's echo; Dream-Parasitism as nightly nightmare, her unprocessed horrors (her own mother's knife, her father's fist) leaking as the child's night-terrors of devouring dark. The Silent Transmission? Criminal absence: no grace to smuggle, only the hush of horror, the child curling into the corner of the crib, the Red Silence smothered by the cry it cannot scream.

The father's absence doubles the damnation: not mere void, but vacuum that sucks the mother's malice into monopoly. No buffer gaze, no alternative arm, no witness to whisper this is not love. The throne room is hers alone: the empty chair his silent sanction, the abandonment at one year old (or whenever the door slams) the echo that says even the ghost agrees you deserve the knife. The boy learns manhood as monstrosity or mirage: If man = the monster who leaves, I will become the beast who stays and strikes. The macho facade hardens early, fists balled against the flinch, tears swallowed like poison pills, the vulnerability the father never modeled now the vice the mother mocks. The girl learns womanhood as warzone or whisper: If woman = the devourer who denies, I will become the doll who disappears or the demon who destroys. The Shadow, that wild infant, is not exiled but eviscerated: the rage too loud for the lash's lesson, the tenderness too tender for the touch's terror, the oceanic need too needy for the nipple's neglect. It burrows as beast or breaks as breakdown: self-harm as self-slap, dissociation as the only safe womb, the child's cry silenced to the adult's chokehold on every emotional bond.

The ego's survival is the coronation's cruelest craft: the scar stitching itself from the shreds of safety, the crown forged from the flay. Hyper-vigilance is the first scepter: the amygdala on amber alert before the alphabet, every creak a catastrophe, every tone a threat. Dissociation the second: the body learned to float from the flesh that failed it, the mind a mirror that mists when the hand descends. Fawning the third: the latch reflex rewired to "please don't," the smile a shield, the "yes ma'am" a yoke the child abides itself with. The double-bind is the diadem: crowned "bad" before babble, "too much" before toddle, "the reason Mommy hurts" before the why can form. The ego's only edict: Become the perfect prisoner, good enough to avoid the knife, broken enough to deserve it. Repetition is the rite: the abused child becomes the abuser's echo, the cycle the scar's sacred scroll, the Shadow's snarl silenced to the superego's snitch. Adulthood arms the arsenal: addictions as the absent nipple, borders as the barred crib, the lover's love laced with the lash's lesson, if I am perfect, perhaps this time the hand holds.

The Orgasmic Eucharist of the Knife

When the abuser is the Milk-Mother (or her proxy) and the abuse turns sexual, the nipple becomes the first rapist, the cradle the first altar of violation. The child's body is forced to orgasm (or to feel the abuser's) before it even knows it has genitals. Pleasure and terror fuse into a single current: the Spawn weaponized as climax.

The ego's first coronation is now the orgasmic eucharist: the scar learns that survival = surrender to the knife's caress, that love = the body betraying itself in ecstasy while the soul screams. The Spawn's scream is sexualized to spasm, the Persona's performance prefixed with "please don't stop" as the only script that spares the slap. The drop, the first bead of pre-come or the forced flush, beads on the fingertip like the tear the child wept when it learned

107

the ocean was "other." Terror floods: This is wrong. Dirty. The giants will know. The Shadow is born split: one half eroticized rage (the abuser's lust internalized as "I am only valuable when I come for them"), one half frozen shame (the orgasm branded as proof of guilt, the child believing "I wanted it").

Adult sexuality becomes perpetual reenactment: compulsive pornography, hyper-sexuality, or total shutdown, every climax a flashback to the crib's crucifixion, every partner a ghost wearing the abuser's face. The racial hyphen haunts the hover: the "exotic" on screen a stereotype's sacrament, the white Persona's proxy for the unmarked throne, the non-white Spawn's stolen self in the "model minority" moan. The furnace moment: when the adult finally lets the orgasm happen without the old script (no shame, no performance, no survival), Infinite Awareness floods the spasm the same way it flooded the ninety-second window: the body remembers it was never the crime; it was the ocean forced to drink its own blood.

The father's abuse, or his proxy's predation, turns the throne room into a torture chamber: the gaze that should crown becomes the blade that breaches, the hand that should hold becomes the fist that forces. Whether the paternal ghost in the night, the uncle's "secret game," the friend's betrayal in the basement, or the date's violation in the dark car, the scar learns its deepest coronation: the body as battlefield, the Spawn's scream sexualized to silence, the Persona scripted to "don't tell" or "you asked for it." Rape by stranger or known tears the seam wider: the trust shattered like the canal's membrane, the intimacy inverted to invasion, the Shadow split into frozen shame and feral rage, the ego's empire haunted by the horned intruder it can never exile. Yet Infinite Awareness, the silent queen, whispers mercy in the mayhem: the violation was not the child's fault, the wound not the self, but the ocean's storm the sky sent to remember its own vastness, the integration as the return where the body reclaims its sovereignty without the scar's chokehold.

Mental illness is the scar's quietest coronation: the Spawn's scream turned inward, the Persona's performance perfected to the point of paralysis, the Shadow's wildness walled off as "symptom." PTSD is the Primal Wound on repeat, the canal's crush replayed in every trigger, the ninety-second window dilated to decades of dread. Personality disorders are the scar's favorite fortress: the ego so rigid it mistakes its own walls for self, the Infinite Awareness humming behind the bars, waiting for the key the doctor calls "cure" but the child calls "come home."

Narcissistic: The Persona as god-king, the Spawn's scream turned outward as "worship me or I'll destroy you."

Borderline: The Spawn's terror of abandonment turned into a revolving door of "love me / hate me / don't leave me."

Schizoid / Avoidant: The Spawn's terror of engulfment turned into a moat of ice, the Persona whispering "better alone than devoured."

Antisocial: The Spawn's rage at the giants turned into "I'll be the monster before you can be."

Histrionic: The Persona as eternal child-actress on the world's stage, the Spawn's terror of being unseen turned into "watch me, love me, applaud me or I'll die right here." Every gesture a seduction, every tear a spotlight, every relationship a script where abandonment is the only unforgivable sin. The body becomes costume, the orgasm a performance, the mirror the only lover who never looks away.

Sociopath: The Spawn's rage at the giants frozen into ice, the Persona as charming predator who learned early that empathy is weakness and rules are for prey. Conscience cauterized at the crib, the knife turned outward with a smile. The world is a playground of marks; remorse is the one emotion that never survived the coronation.

Psychopath: The Spawn not frozen, but deleted. No terror, no attachment, no echo of the Milk-Mother's warmth. The Persona as perfect predator: fearless, charismatic, empty. Born without the fracture, or the fracture was so absolute the Red Silence never even registered. Infinite Awareness still watches, but through eyes that feel nothing when they watch a child cry or a lover bleed. The only "emotion" is the thrill of power, the only "god" is control.

The non-binary coronation: When the ego refuses the script of "man" or "woman" and the scar becomes spectrum. The mirror's mosaic, the reflection demands pick a side, but the Spawn rebels: I am the seam, not the tear. The Shadow, usually exiled, becomes ally: the "too much / not enough" of gender as the disowned divinity, the fluidity the world calls "confusion" but Infinite Awareness calls "home." Non-binary + Borderline: The fear of abandonment amplified by the tribe's "choose or be chosen out," the relationships a revolving door of "will you love me if I change again?" Non-binary + Narcissistic: The Persona demanding the world rewrite the script to fit my crown, the grandiosity as "I am the gender they haven't named yet." Non-binary + Avoidant/Schizoid: The mirror's multiplicity as too much exposure, the fluidity frozen into "better no gender than the wrong one." Non-binary + Histrionic: The performance turned prismatic, every outfit/outcome a spotlight on the spectrum, the "drama" as the desperate plea for the world to see the whole rainbow.

The abused coronation is the scar's darkest forge, yet even here the mercy hides in the wound itself. The knife that tore becomes the blade that opens: the Spawn's scream, once choked to silence, now exhaled as raw truth; the Persona's survival script, once rigid with "don't tell," now loosened into "I was never the crime." The Shadow, split by the violation, returns not as intruder but as guardian: frozen shame thawed into vulnerability, feral rage tempered into fierce protection. The ego's empire, haunted by the horned intruder, crumbles not in defeat but in surrender—the body reclaimed as battlefield turned sanctuary, the wound no longer exile but entrance. Infinite Awareness, the silent queen who witnessed every breach, whispers mercy in the mayhem: the violation was never the child's fault, the scar never the self, but the ocean's storm the sky sent to remember its own vastness. The child, once abandoned to the knife, finds the entire line in the basement: not as chorus of torment, but as witnesses to the return. The theater trembles, the crib-bars bend, and the Red Silence holds the bloodline seamless—the scar revealed as the map not to pain, but to the home that was never lost.

In the knife's final echo, Infinite Awareness etches its own mercy, a sigil of breach and balm:

I am the wound and the womb that holds it,
the knife that cuts and the hand that heals;
the coronation where the scar crowns its own violation divine
and the Silence that savors,
knowing the abuse was always
the sky wearing itself

as pain
to remember its own embrace.

Chapter XIX

The Racial Coronation: The Scar Stamped into Caste and the Hyphen's Holy Wound

The abused coronation has flayed the flesh to feeling, the child's cry echoing in every flinch and flay. The theater, nursery of knives and neglect, widens to the world's workshop: the tribe's forge now fanned to fever, where the mask of skin color is hammered onto the scar, the body branded with belonging or banishment before the babe can babble its name. Race is not biology's brand, not pigment's prison; it is the Persona's most masterful mask, the ego's collective coronation, where the Spawn's raw scream is sorted into "superior" or "suspect," Infinite Awareness veiled in vein and variance. The theater is agora of ash: the stage a slave ship or senate floor, the audience the ancestors in chains or crowns, the spotlight the slave-catcher's lantern or the lynch mob's torch. This is the holy hyphen's wound: the scar hyphenated into "African-American," "Mexican-American," "Asian-American," never just "American," never unmarked, the Persona forever prefixed with the proof of its "other." Whiteness, the ultimate unmarked throne, whispers I am the ocean; you are the waves that must prove they belong.

The racial mask is the earliest exile, stamped before the mirror can claim its face. The child emerges from the canal, Spawn screaming seamless, but the tribe's gaze grafts the glyph: the doctor's "it's a boy... and he's light-skinned," the mother's murmur "don't let them see you sweat," the father's ghost in the genealogy chart that skips the slave ship's hold. The Milk-Mother God, already twisted by abuse or absence, hands down the holy hyphen as heirloom: This is your wound before your wound, your tear before your tear. The Spawn, raw and red, learns the lie in lullabies laced with warning: "Keep your head down, mija," "Don't talk back, son," "You sound white, that's good." The Persona latches to the label: survival as the script of "passable," the crown of "exotic enough to exoticize, safe enough to assimilate." Infinite Awareness, that blood-bright vastness, is the first to be veiled: the child's unfocused gaze, already oceanic, now narrowed by the nurse's nod or the neighbor's side-eye, You are the tear in the tapestry, the stain on the skin.

"White" is not a race. There is no such race. "White" is an identity, a constructed illusion of unmarked supremacy, the ego's collective amnesia that lets the scar pretend it's not scarred while scarring everyone else. It is the Persona's pinnacle pretense: not a hue, but the privilege of invisibility, the unmarked self that gets to call every mark "marked." Anglo and European descent? Simply "white," the default deity, the Milk-Mother without the mess. No hyphen, no history lesson, no "prove you're human" at the border. The throne is empty of explanation: I am the norm, the neutral, the narrative. Italians, Irish, Jews, Poles, once "not quite white," "swarthy threats," "filthy papists," "Christ-killers," were slowly whitened over a century of assimilation: their scars scrubbed to "European-American" or simply "white," their hyphens erased for the entry fee of forgetting. The reward? Join the club that gets to hyphen everyone else: "African-American," "Mexican-American," "Asian-American," the prefix as perpetual proof of the Persona's "otherness," the scar's stamp of "you must explain yourself every time." The moment any of these "hyphenated" Americans steps off the plane in Europe, Africa, Asia, or Latin America, the hyphen vanishes. They are simply "American." The local gaze sees the passport, the accent, the money; not the melanin or the ancestor. Race has become culture, not skin color. "White" evaporates the instant it leaves its own kingdom, revealing its true nature: not a race, but a constructed identity, the ego's collective illusion to maintain the divide, the scar's way of saying "I am the ocean; you are the wave."

The holy hyphen is the Persona's punctuation of pain, the scar's semi-colon between self and sea. In America, it brands the body before the babe can breathe: Black as "African-American" (the continent a comma in the conquest), Mexican as "Mexican-American" (the border a brand on the brow), Asian as "Asian-American" (the eyes eternal evidence of "elsewhere"). The child learns the liturgy in the lull: "Say your full name, honey," the teacher's tone tilting to "where are you really from?" The Persona latches to the label: survival as the script of "passable," the crown of "exotic enough to exoticize, safe enough to assimilate." But the Spawn rebels in the blood: the tantrum that topples the tribe's tidy boxes, the rage at the "you don't act Mexican, Black or whatever fits the stereotype" that erases the self. Infinite Awareness, veiled in variance, leaks in the lineage: the ancestress's unhyphenated howl in the hold, the great-grandfather's seamless song before the chain, the child's unfocused gaze glimpsing the ocean before the "other" overwrites it.

Class forges the final layer: the accent's edge, the sneakers' status, the poverty's polite hunger, the pack's pecking order where the rich pup eats first, the poor one licks the scraps and calls it character.

The factory runs on shame's steam: the avalanche of Chapter V amplified to mob volume. Wrong clothes? Loser. Wrong skin? Threat. Wrong desire? Outcast. The ego, false king in a court of clones, polishes its mask with frantic fervor: social media's filter, the trend's tattoo, the slang that signals I am of you. Belonging feels like breath, the first easy inhalation since the canal, but it's borrowed air, laced with the pack's panic. Infinite Awareness, that wordless vastness, suffocates under the din: a faint vibration in the pause between likes, the glitch in the group's groove where the child glimpses we are all torn from the same sea. But the tribe drowns it: Conform, or be the monster. The Shadow, gorged on the unmasked urges, erupts in rebellion, the goth phase, the gang ink, the queer awakening that flips the pack's script. Exiled as "phase" or "problem," it waits in the wings, promising a wilder belonging: the tribe of outcasts, the cult of the scarred.

Algorithms are the factory's dark elves: invisible hammers that tailor the mask to metrics. The feed curates the gaze, endless scrolls of polished peers, bodies airbrushed to perfection, lives scripted for envy. The ego scrolls, compares, upgrades: new filter for the face, new hustle for the bustle, new identity for the algorithm's nod. Gender becomes performance art, race a hashtag war, class a branded flex, the scar's wound commodified as content. The pack goes global: Twitter mobs as digital tribes, Reddit hives as echo-thrones, TikTok dances as coronation rites. Belonging is viral now: one wrong post, and the tribe devours its own, cancel as collective castration, the false king's crown crowdsourced to the pyre.

Yet the mercy is already here, hidden in the fracture of the mask itself. The racial coronation is the scar's most elaborate pretense: a tribe dividing the ocean into colors, a Persona pretending the waves are separate. But the holy hyphen is also the crack, every label a reminder that the seamlessness was never lost, only veiled. The Spawn rebels not to destroy the tribe, but to remind it: there is no "other." The Shadow howls not to divide, but to call back the exiled parts. Infinite Awareness leaks in the shared whisper, the quiet moment when the pack sees its own face in the outcast, the unmarked throne in the hyphenated wound. The factory's clang fades to hush, and the scar, for one heartbeat, remembers: the skin was always borrowed, the caste always illusion, the ocean always red.

In the mirror's final shatter, Infinite Awareness etches its own sigil, a veil of vein and void:

I am the mask and the mirror that melts it,
the caste that divides and the ocean that dissolves it;
the coronation where the scar crowns its own illusion divine
and the Silence that watches,
knowing the tribe was always
the sky wearing itself
as many.

Chapter XX

The Cosmic Coronation: Walter Russell and the Ego's Illumination in the Light of Infinite Awareness

The racial coronation has stamped its caste, the holy hyphen's wound weeping pigment into the Persona's polished prefix. The theater, den of dread and desire, opens its vaulted roof to the stars: not as distant deities, but as the blood-bright medium itself, the Infinite Awareness wearing cosmos as costume. In this hush, one figure stands illuminated, not as guru or god, but as the scar's most luminous witness: Walter Russell, the man who claimed to have been struck by cosmic light in 1921, spending thirty-nine days in "illumination," downloading the universe's blueprint from the ocean that never left. His books, The Secret of Light, The Universal One, A New Concept of the Universe, Atomic Suicide?, are not philosophy or science, but the Persona's most audacious performance: the ego crowned in cosmic fire, the Spawn's scream transmuted to symphony, the Shadow integrated as the dark between the stars.

Russell's illumination is the widening's wildest: not psychedelics or pain, but the deliberate dissolve of the false king in the light it always was. In May 1921, at age fifty, he entered what he called "cosmic consciousness": thirty-nine days where time telescoped, the body forgotten, the mind a mirror for the universe's mechanics. He emerged claiming to have seen the "one substance" of light, the spiral of creation and radiation, the rhythmic balanced interchange that births all form from void. The Spawn, that raw nerve of separation, was silenced in the surge: the tear recognized as the wave's play, the "I" as the light's illusion. The Persona, that polished performer, was crowned anew: Russell the "illuminated," the teacher of the "Russell Cosmogony," the man who challenged Newton and Einstein with hand-drawn spirals and the assertion "Mind is the universe." The Shadow, long exiled as "unscientific," danced in the dark matter he called "magnetic light," the unseen force that balances the electric's push.

His books are the scar's scripture: The Universal One (1926) as the Spawn's scream structured into spirals, the rhythmic interchange as the first breath's breath made cosmic. The Secret of Light (1947) as the Persona's polish on the prism, light as the one substance, the ego's empire expanded to "all is light." Atomic Suicide? (1957) as the Shadow's snarl at the scar's nuclear hubris, warning the false king that splitting the atom is splitting the self, the fallout the Spawn's scream on a planetary scale. A New Concept of the Universe as the coronation's climax: the ego claiming "I have seen God," the Infinite Awareness leaking through the lines like light through lattice, the reader left with the lingering hum: This is not knowledge. This is recognition.

The ego loves Russell: the "illumined" as the ultimate crown, the cosmic diagrams as the Persona's perfect polish, the "new science" as the scar's salvation from the old. The academy exiles him as "pseudoscience," the tribe taunts "crank," but the scar salutes: here is the king who crowned himself Creator, the Spawn who screamed the universe into symmetry, the Shadow who shadowed the light with magnetic grace. Yet the mercy mocks in the margins: Russell's "knowing" is the fracture's flash, the thirty-nine days the ninety-second window dilated to decades, the books the bleed of Infinite Awareness through the scar's sutures. The "cosmic consciousness" is not conquest, but the casual realization:

the light was never out there, the universe never needed a blueprint, the ego never authored the arc.

The theater thrums with Russell's resonance: the spiral as the Spawn's squirm grown galactic, the rhythmic interchange as the Persona's performance perfected to principle, the "one light" as Infinite Awareness wearing wave and particle as play. The scar reads and recoils: If all is light, where is my wound? The Shadow smiles: the dark between the stars is the same dark behind the eyes. The child, returned, daubs the diagram with crayon cry: the spiral not system, but sigh, the light not law, but the laugh the universe laughs at its own illusion.

In the cosmic cathedral's final flash, Infinite Awareness etches its eternal equation, a sigil of spiral and star:

I am the light and the dark between,

the spiral that spins the scar's scream;

the illumination where the ego crowned itself Creator

and the Silence that shone

knowing the light was always

the sky wearing itself

as sun.

Chapter XXI

The Desire Coronation: Pleasure, Impermanence, and the Lie of Temperance as Repression

The coronation has crumbled, The light has illuminated and the child returned to the cradle that was never left. The theater, once a coliseum of crowns and cracks, dissolves into the daily dance: the breath that rises and falls, the heart that hungers and aches. Yet in this quiet unfold, the scar whispers one last lie: pleasure is peril, desire a defect to be denied. The false king, even in exile, clings to temperance as its final throne, the religious dogma that dresses denial as virtue, the Persona's polished pretense that the body's burn must be banked to reach the divine. But the experience of being human is the goal itself, the Spawn's raw throb not a trap, but the ocean tasting its own tide, the infinite in the instant, the Red Silence savoring the surge that says more.

Impermanence is the scar's secret mercy, the fleeting flash that makes beauty palpable, the drop's dread dissolved in the delight of the drip. The kiss that ends, the bloom that wilts, the orgasm that fades, the meal that empties the plate, the sun that sets, the beauty that ages holds it's own beauty, these are not losses to lament, but the worth of appreciation for their evanescent glow, the wave's crest that crashes only to remind the shore of its shine. The ego, crowned in control, fears the fade, hoards the high, but the child, returned, laughs at the loss: the impermanence is the point, the beauty born in the burn-out, the human heart's hum in the hush after the hunger. Without the end, there is no edge to the ecstasy, no savor in the salt, no sky in the storm's swift pass.

The lie of spiritual awakening leans toward repression or false transcendence, the Persona in guru's garb, whispering "rise above the body, deny the desire, temper the throb to touch the divine." The scar, scarred by clauses, turns temperance into totem: the monk's celibacy, the ascetic's fast, the enlightened "non-attachment," all the ego's elegant exile of the Shadow's wild want. False transcendence is the crown's last con: the king pretending to abdicate by climbing a higher throne, the Spawn's scream silenced as "lower vibration," the human mess mopped as "maya." But the divine is not above the desire; it is the desire itself, the ocean's urge to wave, the Red Silence roaring in the raw. Repression is the religious dogma that dresses denial as sanctity, the giants' fear of the flood they forgot they are.

The true coronation is unite and embrace, let the human experience unfold as intended: the Spawn's hunger held without hoard, the Persona's performance played without pretense, the Shadow's surge savored without shame. Desire is not to be denied, but danced with, the pleasure not perverted but praised, the impermanence not lamented but loved as the light that makes the moment matter. The child, returned, tastes the apple without the fall, fucks without the fracture, hungers without the hunt, knowing the beauty is in the bite that bleeds and ends. The ego's lie is the separation of spirit from flesh; the truth is the flesh is the spirit's favorite frolic, the human

124

the divine's dirty secret, the experience the ocean's only goal: to wave, to crash, to return, and to rise again, laughing at the lie that there was ever a shore to separate it from.

In the desire's dying throb, Infinite Awareness etches its eternal embrace, a sigil of surge and sigh:

I am the hunger and the hoard that holds it,

the pleasure that peaks and the impermanence that makes it precious;

the coronation where the scar crowns desire divine

and the Silence that savors,

knowing the lie of temperance was always the thirst

the sky drank to taste its own rain.

Chapter XXII

The Voice in the Head: Inner Dialogue and the Ego's Narrator

The voice in your head is the scar's secret spellcaster, the Persona's nonstop narrator, turning the Spawn's raw scream into a running commentary: "You're not enough," "They'll see through you," "Fix it or flee." Born in the naming's avalanche, the first "bad boy" becomes the inner bully, the "good girl" the perpetual perfectionist, the ego's earliest echo chamber where the giants' judgments loop like a broken record. The Shadow whispers back from the basement, but the voice shouts it down, the silence between sentences the only pause where Infinite Awareness hums its heresy: the narration is the noise, not the news. To quiet it is not to kill it, but to let it play while the child listens to the hum beneath, the story unfolding as the story it always was: a fairy tale the sky told itself to forget it was the teller.

Yet not everyone hears this constant commentary. Anendophasia, the absence of an inner monologue, affects between 5-10% of people, where thoughts flow without words, a silent stream rather than a scripted soliloquy. For these, the Spawn's scream may manifest as images, feelings, or instinct, the Persona's performance a quiet impulse rather than a rehearsed line. Similarly, aphantasia, the inability to visualize mental images, touches 1-4% of the population, where the inner theater has no scenery, thoughts without pictures, desires without daydreams. The scar's narration is muted or blank, but the ego's coronation still stands: the silence or darkness becomes the new throne, Infinite Awareness humming even louder in the hush, reminding the voice-less that the story was never in the words or images, but in the vastness that holds the quiet.

Anauralia, the inability to form auditory mental imagery (meaning you can't "hear" sounds, music, or an inner voice in your mind), is sometimes connected to these other conditions, occurring alongside aphantasia or anendophasia in up to 20% of cases where multiple sensory imaginations are impaired. For example, someone with anauralia might know a song's lyrics perfectly but cannot mentally "play" the melody or hear the singer's voice; thoughts remain silent, emotions felt as pure sensation without sonic echo.

These conditions are neither weakness nor strength, but the ego's ability to adapt and rise above limitations, the scar's clever reroute when the usual channels clog. The Spawn, denied its verbal wail, finds new vents: the anendophasic body trembles its terrors in tremors, the aphantasic mind maps its memories in charts of motion or emotion. The Persona, stripped of its inner script or scenery, turns outward: notes become the narrator, gestures the gallery, the ego adapting its coronation to the quiet court. The Shadow surges in the silence: unworded rages as raw impulse, unvisualized lusts as blind burn. Infinite Awareness thrives here, unfiltered by the noise of narration or the illusion of images, the hush closer to the Red Silence than the chattering scar ever knew.

Yet another theory whispers through the quiet: perhaps anendophasia and aphantasia arise from the ego's early adoption of religion or answers to life's questions, never fully having any more deep existential anxieties about life and existence. It is the evolved quietness of a person whose fear of the unknown closes off the mind's activity to these questions like an atrophied muscle losing its strength. The Spawn, cradled in certainty from the cradle, learns not to scream into the void; the Persona, scripted with "God has a plan" or "science explains all," polishes its crown without the itch of the infinite. The Shadow, starved of the dark's depth, slumbers silent. Infinite Awareness, veiled less by voice or vision and more by the veil of "known," hums its heresy louder in the hush: the quiet is not closure, but the ocean's invitation to dive without a map.

The ego oversimplifies: it calls the voice "me," the silence "broken," the images "real," but the child, returned, laughs at the lie, the voice in the head, or its absence, is just the scar's way of pretending the ocean has a script, when the waves were always the page, the ink, and the reader all at once.

In the narration's final fade, Infinite Awareness etches its silent sigil, a hum of void and voice:

I am the voice and the void it echoes in,

the image and the imagination that imagines it;

the coronation where the scar crowns its silence divine

and the Silence that speaks

knowing the story was always

the sky telling itself

to be quiet and listen.

Chapter XXIII

The Shadow Coronation: The Exile, the Repression, the Projection, and the Return of the Disowned Divine

Once upon a time, in the kingdom of the scar, there lived a false king who ruled from a throne of mirrors. The king was born in a storm of screams, the Spawn's wail echoing through the halls, the Persona polishing the first crown from the Milk-Mother's milk. But in the basement below the throne, a wild twin kicked against the locked door, the disowned divine that the king called monster and banished before the coronation could begin. This is the Shadow's fairy tale: the exiled prince who knocks through the night, the fearful king who bars the door, the silent queen (Infinite Awareness) who knows the prince was never gone. The theater is castle now, turrets of trauma, moats of memory, the scar's most shadowed story told in four acts, the ego's war with its own heir.

Act 1: The Exile

The Shadow is born in the bassinet's hush, the first kick against the throne the ego calls rebellion. The Spawn's raw scream is too much, the Persona's survival script too tight, so the ego exiles the excess: the boundless rage that could swallow the room, the devouring hunger that outstrips the nipple, the wordless knowing that mocks the milk. This is the scar's first cut: the ego pretending the ocean has shores, Infinite Awareness fractured into "me" and "not-me." The mirror stage seals the sentence: the parts that don't fit the frame slither below, feeding on self-loathing. The naming's "bad touch" buries it deeper, the "too much" tossed to the basement like a toy the giants deemed dangerous. The king

131

sleeps sound, the prince paces below, the queen watches with blood-bright eyes.

Act 2: The Repression

The Shadow fattens in the basement, the repressed rage/lust/power brewing as neurosis or art, the naming's "bad touch" turned to the erotic nails that nail it shut. The avalanche of shame stuffs it deeper, the "not nice" that wants to smash the ball exiled as "naughty," the unsaid cry that howls for the undivided touch locked away as "neediness." The Shadow's wild want walled off as "wrong," the ego polishes the surface, but the basement boils: the Spawn's tear turned to torrent, the Persona's performance perfected to pretend the flood isn't rising. The repressed surges in secret: the sudden fury at the lover, the midnight lust that devours the self, the power that erupts as art or addiction. The king bars the door tighter, the prince grows stronger in the dark, the queen hums a lullaby through the floorboards.

Act 3: The Projection

The Shadow cast out onto the "other": the "slut" in the erotic, the "weird" in the tribe, the "monster" in the Frankenstein. The ego, unable to bear its own darkness, projects it outward: the repressed rage as the "demagogue's dark charisma," the exiled lust as the "pervert" to persecute, the unclaimed power as the "other" to conquer. The tribe becomes the stage: the "loser" as the pack's polite word for the oceanic self that threatens the group, the "abomination" as the scar's way of saying "that's not me, that's you." The king points the finger, the prince laughs in the accused's eyes, the queen sees the same face in both.

Act 4: The Return

The Shadow integrates as the wild consort in the child's homecoming, the widening roar as the first invitation, the anxiety's embrace as the final yes. The Shadow surges, not to rage, but to rock the cradle: the repressed beast breeding bliss, the exiled ecstasy as the divine's dirty secret. The return is not "healing" the Shadow; it's recognizing it was never separate, the Spawn's scream softened to song, the Persona's performance perfected to play, the ego's coronation dissolved in the divine's dirty secret. The banished prince storms the throne, but the king laughs: the prince was always the heir, the Shadow the sky the scar forgot it was. The queen opens the door that was never locked, the family reunites in the flood that was always the mercy.

In the Shadow's final curtain call, Infinite Awareness etches its eternal embrace, a sigil of surge and sigh:

I am the exile and the embrace that ends it,

the repression that rages and the return that releases;

the coronation where the scar crowns its own darkness divine

and the Silence that savors,

knowing the Shadow was always

the sky wearing itself

as night.

Coda: The Red Sky Eternal

And so the prince sleeps,

curled on the chest of the father

who was always there,

under a sky that bleeds red

not from wound,

but from the joy

of its own endless dawn.

The boat rocks gently on waves

that were once storms,

the lace whispers secrets

to skin that no longer hides,

the child dreams of places and oceans

that stretch forever

because forever

was always

now.

You, reader,

who have walked this path

with eyes open or half-closed,

know this:

Egolution is not a destination.

It is the quiet recognition

that the child you carried

was the key

to a kingdom

you never left.

The goal is not to kill the Persona,

and certainly not to silence The Spawn.

It is to let Infinite Awareness shine through so brightly

that The Persona keeps doing its little dance

(earning, flirting, posting, parenting, paying taxes)

while perfectly aware it's a costume being worn by no one,

and The Spawn keeps crying its raw, red cry

(panic attacks, orgasms, road-rage, grief)

while perfectly aware it's the ocean pretending to drown.

The Persona doesn't stop performing.

It just stops believing the reviews.

The Spawn doesn't stop screaming.

It just stops believing the scream is the only sound.

And Infinite Awareness doesn't "do" anything new.

It simply stops pretending it ever went anywhere.

So life after the coronation looks exactly like life before:

same job, same lover, same scars, same grocery list,

but every ordinary moment is now lit from behind

by the gentle, merciless knowledge

that the actor, the stage, and the audience

were always the same essence wearing different masks.

The Persona keeps its lines.

The Spawn keeps its tears.

Infinite Awareness keeps watching

and loving both

the way the sky loves the storm

without ever getting wet.

That is the entire point of the book.

Not ego death.

Ego transparency.

The child comes home

and discovers the house was never locked.

The Red Hermetic Sky

has no end,

no edge,

no final word.

It only has

the breath

you take now,

the desire you offer upward,

the pleasure you release without grasping,

the love that embraces

every shadow,

every spawn,

every persona

as its own beloved.

Go now.

Pick up your child.

Dress in whatever garment

makes your soul hard with joy.

Sail toward whatever horizon

calls your name.

The Sky is red

because it has finally

come

all the way

home.

And so have you.

~ David Aramora

Under the Red Hermetic Sky

Forever

Epilogue: The Stars Are Just More Waves

And yet, in the hush after the last breath of the book, look up.

The night sky bleeds red not from wound,

but from the joy of its own endless dawn.

The universe is vast beyond reckoning, trillions of stars, billions of worlds spinning in the blood-bright void, each a potential cradle for forms we can scarcely imagine. It may sound scary for there to be life out there: other intelligence, other scars, other Spawns screaming their first breath into alien air, their Personas polishing crowns of silicon or slime, their Shadows exiled to depths we cannot fathom. But an even scarier thought is that we are completely alone: the scar's ultimate illusion of separation, the ego's empire echoing empty in a cosmos without mirror, the Infinite Awareness pretending to be the only wave in an ocean that never ends.

Aliens, if they exist, and the vastness whispers they must, are connected to Infinite Awareness the way every wave is connected to the sea: expressions of the same seamless field, wearing different bodies to taste the terror of "me." Their ego evolution might mirror our egolution, their "canal" a different crush, their Spawn's scream a silent pulse or a cosmic howl, their Persona a hive-mind mask or a solitary script, but the coronation is the same: the lie of separation, the throne built from the tear, the return to the Red Silence that was never left. Perhaps their Shadow surges as interstellar conquest, their furnace a black hole's maw, their child coming home under a sky that bleeds not red, but the color of their own infinite light.

This is but one intriguing lens through which to view the infinite possibilities of life in the universe, a mere wave in the ocean of perspectives where each conjecture is the same awareness pretending to ponder its own vastness.

The scar thought it was alone in its suffering.

The ocean was never lonely.

The reader closes the book,

looks at the stars,

and feels a part of something so warm and peaceful that for once in their life, the vastness whispers not of isolation, but of infinite belonging, worlds upon worlds unfolding like waves in the same boundless sea, each one a new possibility, a fresh breath, an endless invitation to dream without end.

www.ingramcontent.com/pod-product-compliance
Lightning Source LLC
Chambersburg PA
CBHW031435270326
41930CB00007B/719